# SHARE WHAT YOU KNOW:

## WRITING AND SELF-PUBLISHING FOR ENTREPRENEURS

THE SUCCESSFUL SELF-PUBLISHER SERIES
BOOK FIVE

## RAE A. STONEHOUSE

LIVE FOR EXCELLENCE PRODUCTIONS

**ISBN - E-book:** 978-1-998813-44-5

**ISBN – Paperback:** 978-1-998813-49-0

**ISBN – Audiobook:** 978-1-998813-46-9

# INTRODUCTION

Are you an entrepreneur, business leader, or expert with valuable insights to share? Do you aspire to establish yourself as a thought leader in your field? The world needs your unique perspective. Self-publishing offers an accessible pathway to make your voice heard.

Discover the transformative power of writing and self-publishing.

Welcome to Book Five in the Successful Self-Publisher Series: **Share What You Know: Writing and Self-Publishing for Entrepreneurs.**

In this comprehensive guide, we will unlock the immense potential of writing and self-publishing to grow your personal brand, strengthen your business, and make a genuine impact. You will learn proven techniques to craft compelling stories that resonate with readers. We provide step-by-step guidance to professionally publish and powerfully market your book.

This book will reveal:

- How to identify your distinctive author voice to create authentic and engaging stories

- Structuring techniques to organize your ideas into an outline that flows logically
- Editing methods to refine your manuscript and elevate the quality of your writing
- Options for visually appealing book covers and interiors that represent your brand
- Distribution strategies to make your book available to the widest possible readership
- Marketing tactics to spread awareness, connect with readers, and drive book sales
- Monetization opportunities to generate revenue streams beyond book sales
- Platform-building advice to prove yourself to be an authority in your niche
- Relationship-nurturing strategies to foster a devoted readership that champions your work

Whether you are an entrepreneur, business owner, executive, or simply someone with valuable insights to share, this book will empower you to self-publish your unique story and amplify your message. Our proven techniques and strategic advice will help you engage readers, enrich lives, and advance your professional goals.

This book is all about showing you the way to success. Each chapter builds on the last, offering fresh insights and new skills. It's designed to be a journey, so buckle up and read it from start to finish the first time. Later, come back to it and find the parts that speak to you the most.

As in my previous books, some ideas might come back in different chapters, but each time with a new twist. That's how we grow – by looking at things from various angles.

Factual case studies have been included to illustrate points. In addition, fictional stories have been added to breathe life into theoretical ideas, offering an imaginative exploration of potential real-world applications and implications.

# INTRODUCTION

The time is now to take control of your story and make an impact. Read on to begin your transformative self-publishing journey.

Welcome, and happy writing!

Rae A. Stonehouse

August 2023

CHAPTER ONE

# UNDERSTANDING THE POWER OF WRITING & SELF-PUBLISHING FOR BUSINESS GROWTH

## THE INCREASING POPULARITY of Self-Publishing as A Powerful Tool for Entrepreneurs in The Digital Age:

In the digital age, self-publishing has emerged as a powerful tool for entrepreneurs, enabling them to share their knowledge with a global audience. With the increasing popularity of e-books and digital platforms, self-publishing has become more accessible, affordable, and efficient, revolutionizing the way entrepreneurs communicate and connect with their target market.

One of the primary reasons for the growing popularity of self-publishing among entrepreneurs is the ability to maintain complete control over their content and creative vision. Unlike traditional publishing, where authors must often compromise on their ideas to cater to the publisher's preferences, self-publishing lets entrepreneurs keep full autonomy. This empowers them to communicate their message in an authentic and personalized manner, fostering a stronger connection with their readership.

Additionally, self-publishing offers entrepreneurs an incredible speed to market. With traditional publishing, the process from submission to publication can take months or even years. Conversely, self-publishing lets entrepreneurs write, format, and publish their work within a matter of days or weeks. This agility enables them to respond to market trends and timely issues, proving themselves to be thought leaders in their respective industries.

Self-publishing provides entrepreneurs with a greater share of the profits. In a traditional publishing model, authors often receive a relatively small percentage of the book sales, with the majority going to publishers, distributors, and bookstores. Conversely, by self-publishing, entrepreneurs can earn a significantly higher royalty rate, directly affecting their bottom line and providing them with a more lucrative revenue stream.

Self-publishing lets entrepreneurs tap into a global market. With digital platforms like Amazon Kindle, Apple Books, and Smashwords, entrepreneurs can reach readers all around the world, eliminating the limitations of geographic boundaries. This broad reach not only enhances the exposure and visibility of their work but also provides opportunities to connect with a diverse audience, expanding their network and potential customer base.

Self-publishing has gained increasing popularity as a powerful tool for entrepreneurs in the digital age due to its ability to provide creative control, rapid speed to market, increased profit share, and global reach. As technology continues to advance and access to digital publishing platforms becomes even more seamless, entrepreneurs are empowered to leverage self-publishing as a strategic avenue to share their ideas, build their personal brand, and drive business success.

### Lever The Power of Self-Publishing: The Significance of Aligning Publishing Goals with Business Objectives for Entrepreneurs

In recent years, self-publishing has emerged as a game-changer for entrepreneurs and creative individuals looking to share their work with the world. Unlike traditional publishing methods, self-publishing offers unique advantages and opportunities that can help entrepreneurs in multiple ways. This section will explore some of the key advantages, including creative control, faster publishing process, and higher profit margins.

One of the most significant advantages of self-publishing is the degree of creative control it offers to entrepreneurs. In traditional publishing, authors must often compromise on their artistic vision to align with the preferences and market demands of publishing houses. However, self-publishing empowers entrepreneurs to maintain complete control over their work. They can decide on the content, design, format, and cover art. This creative freedom enables authors to express their unique voice, experiment with different genres, and take risks that might not be possible through traditional publishing channels. By maintaining creative control, entrepreneurs can truly showcase their talents and present their work exactly as they envision it.

Another advantage that self-publishing brings to entrepreneurs is a faster publishing process. Traditional publishing can be a slow and daunting process involving finding agents or publishers, convincing them of the book's potential, negotiating contracts, and following various editorial timelines. But self-publishing eliminates these hurdles, letting entrepreneurs bring their work to the market quickly. With self-publishing platforms like Amazon Kindle Direct Publishing and Lulu, entrepreneurs can publish their books within days or even hours. This faster publishing process enables them to capitalize on time-sensitive topics, trends, or events, ensuring relevant and timely content for their target audience.

Self-publishing often leads to higher profit margins, which is a significant advantage for entrepreneurs seeking financial gains from their work. In traditional publishing, authors typically receive a modest royalty percentage that is significantly lower than the sale price of each book. Additionally, there are various deductions, such as agent fees, marketing expenses, and publisher's commissions. Conversely, self-published authors can keep a larger share of the profits. With the lower overhead costs associated with self-publishing, entrepreneurs can enjoy higher profit margins per book sale, maximizing their returns on investment. This additional financial flexibility can provide entrepreneurs with more opportunities to reinvest in their future projects or expand their business.

Self-publishing offers unique advantages and opportunities to entrepreneurs. The creative control it provides lets entrepreneurs express their artistic vision without compromise. The faster publishing process enables timely releases and quicker access to the market. Self-publishing often leads to higher profit margins, giving entrepreneurs more financial flexibility. With these benefits, self-publishing has become an avenue for entrepreneurial creativity, letting individuals share their work with the world on their own terms and reap the rewards of their efforts.

### Case Studies and Success Stories of Entrepreneurs Who Have Used Self-Publishing to Grow Their Personal Brand & Achieve Business Success:

### Case Study 1: Amanda Hocking - From Self-Published Author to Millionaire

Amanda Hocking, a young writer from Minnesota, is one of the most notable success stories in self-publishing. In 2010, she self-published her paranormal romance novels on platforms like Amazon Kindle, bypassing traditional publishing routes. Despite facing many rejections from literary agents and publishing houses, Hocking's books quickly gained popularity among readers, and she became the first self-published author to sell over one million copies.

Hocking used social media and various online platforms to market her books and engage with her growing fan base. Her ability to consistently deliver high-quality, captivating stories helped her build a strong personal brand within the fantasy and romance genres. As her readership increased, Hocking gradually expanded her personal brand beyond writing, securing lucrative book deals, movie options, and merchandising opportunities. Today, she is recognized as a successful entrepreneur who used self-publishing as a steppingstone to achieve both personal and business success.

SHARE WHAT YOU KNOW:

## Case Study 2: Mark Dawson - Building an Empire through Self-Publishing

Mark Dawson, a former lawyer turned thriller author from the United Kingdom, used self-publishing to leverage his personal brand and build a thriving business empire. Dawson self-published his first book in 2013 and faced initial challenges like low sales and lack of visibility. However, he quickly identified the importance of marketing and advertising his books to reach a wider audience.

His John Milton thriller series became a huge hit, letting him quit his day job in 2013.

Dawson successfully harnessed the power of social media and online advertising platforms to promote his books directly to his target audience. By tracking and optimizing his marketing efforts, he scaled his sales significantly.

Dawson has since expanded his personal brand as a self-publishing guru. He founded Self-Publishing Formula to teach others his marketing methods through online courses and events. He also co-founded the Self-Publishing Show podcast. Dawson now runs a multi-million-dollar self-publishing business empire, exemplifying how intellectual property and personal branding can create entrepreneurial success.

Through strategic marketing, consistent content creation, and brand building, Dawson transformed his self-publishing venture into a highly profitable business. He now earns a large income from both his books and the products and services he offers aspiring authors.

## Case Study 3: Michael Anderle - From Corporate Job to Full-Time Author

Michael Anderle worked in the corporate world but dreamed of becoming an author. While working his day job, he self-published his first fantasy novel in 2016 and created a fantasy series called The Kurtherian Gambit. He had a goal of writing 20 books that would generate $50,000 in annual revenue, but he exceeded his expectations and earned over $10,000 in monthly income within just three months of publishing.

He continued to release more books and grow his fan base, and by 2018, he had over 60 titles and a 7-figure annual income from his self-publishing business. He also founded his own publishing company, LMBPN Publishing, that focuses on author collaboration and co-writing.

**Case Study 4: Jill Smith - Leveraging a Self-Published Book to Market her Coaching Business** (This story is a fictional example for illustrative purposes)

Jill Smith started her life coaching business in 2015 after struggling with burnout and lack of fulfillment in her corporate career. Within a few years, Jill built a steady client base and an income of $60,000 yearly through her one-on-one coaching services. However, she wanted to scale her business further.

In 2019, Jill decided to self-publish a book detailing her personal journey and the coaching techniques she used to find purpose and balance in life. She titled it "Living with Intention: A Guide to Crafting a Meaningful Life". Jill used the book as a lead magnet, offering free copies in exchange for email sign-ups. This let her rapidly grow her email list.

Jill heavily promoted the book on social media and drove traffic to the landing page through paid ads. She also appeared as a guest on relevant podcasts and was featured in online publications focused on self-help and personal growth.

Within 6 months, Jill had sold over 5,000 copies of her book. Her email list grew from 1,200 to over 15,000 subscribers. Many readers of the book signed up for her coaching services, increasing her income to over $250,000 that year.

By strategically leveraging a self-published book, Jill established herself as a thought leader in her field. The book served as a powerful marketing tool to drive awareness of her coaching business and attract ideal clients. Within a year, Jill scaled her business revenue over 4x through the leverage provided by her book.

**Here are comments from Jill on her journey:**

When I first decided to write and self-publish a book, it represented a major leap of faith. Leaving the safety net of my corporate career to start a coaching business was scary enough. Writing a book based on my personal experiences felt vulnerable and risky. However, the process was one of the most rewarding decisions I've made.

Writing Living with Intention forced me to examine my own journey and codify the lessons I learned about finding purpose. The experience crystallized my coaching methods and enabled me to share it with a wider audience. By opening up about my own struggles, I connected with readers on a deeper level. The feedback I received showed me that my story resonated with people craving more meaning and fulfillment.

Promoting the book tested my comfort zone. I had to step up my online presence and proactively contact the media. But the hard work paid off. The book provided credibility and opened doors to new opportunities like podcast interviews. My email list grew exponentially, letting me educate people about my coaching services. Within months, book sales and new clients helped me take my business to the next level.

This experience taught me the power of thought leadership. By generously sharing my own experiences, I built a reputable brand and position myself as an expert. The leverage provided by the book fueled rapid growth for my business. It took courage to put my story out there, but doing so let me scale my impact and income dramatically. Writing Living with Intention was a defining moment in my entrepreneurial journey. Stepping outside my comfort zone opened up new possibilities for my career and enabled me to help change many more lives through my coaching.

~

These case studies highlight the potential for entrepreneurial success through self-publishing. By embracing self-publishing platforms and leveraging their personal brand, both Amanda Hocking and Mark Dawson grew their businesses, expand their offerings, and achieve significant financial success. Their stories serve as inspiration for aspiring entrepreneurs looking to use self-publishing to achieve their business goals.

**Maximizing the Impact and Value of Published Content: The Crucial Role of Aligning Self-Publishing Goals with Broad Business Objectives:**

Self-publishing has emerged as a powerful avenue for individuals and businesses to share their knowledge, stories, and knowledge with a wider audience. However, to make the most of this opportunity and make sure the published content creates maximum impact and value, it is crucial to align self-publishing goals with overarching business goals.

One of the primary reasons for aligning self-publishing goals with business objectives is to create a cohesive and consistent brand image. Businesses carefully craft their brand identities to resonate with their target audience, and published content should reflect and reinforce these brand values. Whether it is a thought leadership book or a how-to guide related to the business, the content should align with the company's mission, vision, and values. This helps in establishing the business as an authority in their industry and builds trust among readers.

Another key aspect of aligning self-publishing goals with business objectives is to drive real results. Publishing content can provide opportunities for lead generation, customer acquisition, and even revenue generation. By aligning the goals of self-publishing with these overarching business objectives, individuals and businesses can strategically plan their content to cater to their target audience's needs and preferences. This approach not only maximizes the impact of the published content but also makes sure it delivers measurable results, such as increased website traffic, higher conversion rates, or enhanced brand recognition.

Aligning self-publishing goals with business objectives helps in reaching the right audience effectively. Self-publishing offers a vast range of platforms and distribution channels to share content. By understanding the target market and demographic, it becomes easier to choose the most suitable platforms to promote the published content. For example, if the goal is to reach professionals and decision-makers in a specific industry, publishing on platforms like LinkedIn or industry-specific forums can be more impactful compared to general e-book publishing websites. This targeted approach makes sure the content reaches the desired audience, maximizing its value and impact.

Additionally, aligning self-publishing goals with business objectives makes sure the published content supports broader marketing and promotional efforts. Content can be repurposed across various marketing channels such as social media, email newsletters, and blog posts. By aligning the themes and messages of the published content with the overall marketing strategy, businesses can create a cohesive and engaging brand experience for their audience. The published content becomes an integral part of the marketing efforts, supporting the brand's positioning and driving consistent messaging across different platforms.

Aligning self-publishing goals with overarching business objectives is crucial to maximize the impact and value of the published content. By creating a cohesive brand image, driving real results, reaching the right audience effectively, and supporting broader marketing efforts, individuals and businesses can harness the potential of self-publishing to its fullest extent. When self-publishing is integrated seamlessly into the wider business strategy, it becomes a powerful tool for establishing thought leadership, building brand trust, and driving business growth.

. . .

**Practical Tips & Strategies for Entrepreneurs to Effectively Self-Publish Their Work:**

Self-publishing has become a popular route for entrepreneurs looking to share their knowledge, insights, and experiences with a broader audience. However, successfully self-publishing a book requires careful planning and execution. Here are practical tips and strategies for entrepreneurs to effectively self-publish their work, including writing techniques, editing processes, and marketing methods:

**Define your purpose and target audience:** Before starting the writing process, clarify the purpose of your book and identify the specific audience you want to reach. This will help you shape your content, tone, and style to resonate with your target readers.

**Develop a writing routine:** Establish a consistent writing routine that works for you. Give specific times each day or week dedicated only to writing. Stick to your routine, even if it means writing for a short period each day. Consistency is key to maintaining momentum throughout the writing process.

**Outline your book:** Create a detailed outline or structure for your book before you begin writing. This will serve as a roadmap and help maintain focus during the writing process. Ensure your outline covers all the major sections and chapters you plan to include in your book.

**Write in drafts:** Don't strive for perfection in your initial drafts. Instead, focus on getting your ideas down on paper. Once you have a complete draft, review, and revise it multiple times, improving the organization and flow of your content with each iteration.

**Seek professional editing support:** Self-published books can benefit greatly from professional editing. Hire an editor to review your manuscript for grammar, spelling, structure, and overall coherence. Their expertise can significantly enhance the quality of your work.

**Leverage beta readers:** Connect with a group of beta readers who can offer constructive feedback on your book. This unbiased perspective will help you identify any areas that need improvement and address any potential issues before publishing.

**Design an appealing book cover:** Invest time and resources in creating an eye-catching book cover. A professionally designed cover will attract potential readers and increase the perceived value of your work.

**Create a marketing plan:** Even before the book is published, begin developing a marketing strategy. Identify promotional activities such as blog tours, guest posts, social media campaigns, and paid advertising that will help you build buzz and reach your target audience.

**Use social media and online platforms:** Leverage social media platforms such as LinkedIn, Twitter, Facebook, and Instagram to build your author brand and engage with your audience. Create a professional website or blog to showcase your book, provide updates, and share additional valuable content.

**Leverage your existing network:** Leverage the power of your existing network to promote your book. Contact colleagues, friends, family, and business connections who may be interested in supporting your work. Offer them incentives to help spread the word and generate buzz around your book.

**Explore self-publishing platforms:** Use reputable self-publishing platforms such as Amazon Kindle Direct Publishing (KDP), Smashwords, or IngramSpark to distribute your book in various formats (e-book, print, audiobook). Familiarize yourself with these platforms and follow their guidelines to ensure your book is effectively published and available to a wide audience.

**Consider professional assistance:** If you lack the time or knowledge required for certain parts of self-publishing, consider hiring professionals to help you. This could include cover design, formatting, or even book marketing. Using professional services can save time and ensure a higher-quality end product.

Remember, self-publishing requires determination, persistence, and continuous learning. By using these practical tips and strategies, entrepreneurs can effectively self-publish their work, prove themselves to be thought leaders, and reach their desired audience.

. . .

## Self-Publishing: Building Credibility & Establishing Thought Leadership

Self-publishing has revolutionized the way entrepreneurs can showcase their knowledge, build credibility, and attract new business opportunities. By self-publishing their work, entrepreneurs can establish themselves as industry thought leaders, gaining recognition and enhancing their reputation. This section aims to provide practical tips and strategies for entrepreneurs to effectively self-publish their work, covering writing techniques, editing processes, and marketing methods.

**Choosing the Right Topic:**

Select a topic that aligns with your area of expertise and audience's interests. Conduct thorough research to identify any gaps in the existing literature, letting you stand out as a credible and unique voice within your industry.

**Writing Techniques:**

- Define your goals and target audience before starting the writing process. Consider their needs, preferences, and pain points to provide valuable insights and solutions.
- Develop an outline to structure your work and ensure a logical flow. This will help you maintain coherence and clarity throughout the publication.
- Use clear and concise language, avoiding jargon that might alienate readers. Focus on delivering your message effectively and make complex topics understandable to a wider audience.

**Editing Process:**

- Review your work multiple times, checking for grammar, spelling, and punctuation errors. Ensure your writing is polished and free from any inconsistencies or ambiguities.
- Seek feedback from trusted individuals in your industry or subject matter experts. Their insights will help you refine your work and strengthen your arguments.
- Consider hiring a professional editor who can provide an objective perspective and enhance the overall quality of your publication.

**Publishing Formats and Platforms:**

- Explore different publishing options such as e-books, paperback, or audiobooks, depending on your target audience's preferences.
- Utilize self-publishing platforms like Amazon Kindle Direct Publishing, Smashwords, or Kobo Writing Life to distribute and market your work to a wide audience.
- Create a professional author website or blog to showcase your expertise and provide more resources or insights related to your publication. This helps in building credibility and shows your commitment to your industry.

**Marketing Methods:**

- Leverage your existing professional networks and social media platforms to promote your publication. Share excerpts, insights, or quotes from your work to generate interest and engage with your audience.
- Collaborate with influencers, bloggers, or industry publications to guest post, conduct interviews, or contribute articles. This enables you to tap into their established audience and enhance your thought leadership.

- Engage in public speaking opportunities, such as conferences or webinars, where you can discuss the key themes and ideas discussed in your publication. This further establishes your credibility and attracts new business opportunities.

Self-publishing provides entrepreneurs with a powerful tool to showcase their expertise, build credibility, and attract new business opportunities. By following the practical tips and strategies mentioned above, entrepreneurs can effectively self-publish their work, leveraging strong writing techniques, thorough editing processes, and targeted marketing methods. By building credibility and establishing thought leadership within their industry, entrepreneurs open the doors to new collaborations, speaking engagements, and business opportunities.

**The Future of Self-Publishing for Entrepreneurs:**

The future of self-publishing for entrepreneurs is promising, with emerging trends, technological advancements, and potential challenges shaping the constantly evolving publishing landscape. Here is an overview of what can be expected.

**Emerging Trends:**

**Rise of E-books:** E-books have gained tremendous popularity in recent years and are projected to continue growing. Entrepreneurs can leverage this trend by self-publishing e-books, which offer cost-effective production and distribution, accessibility across various devices, and an increasing customer base.

**Increased Diversity in Content:** With self-publishing, entrepreneurs are no longer limited to traditional publishing gatekeepers. This enables a more diverse range of content, including niche topics, books catering to specific communities, and innovative storytelling techniques.

**Personal Branding and Entrepreneurial Voice:** Self-publishing lets entrepreneurs establish their personal brand and express their entrepreneurial voice through their books. This trend will continue to grow as authors use books to showcase their expertise, market their businesses, or establish thought leadership.

**Technological Advancements:**

**Artificial Intelligence (AI) and Machine Learning:** Advancements in AI and machine learning technologies will aid entrepreneurs in tasks such as grammar and style checks, content editing, and cover design recommendations, streamlining the self-publishing process while reducing cost and effort.

**Print-on-Demand (POD) Technology:** As technology improves, entrepreneurs can take advantage of POD services, which allow for small print runs, reducing inventory costs and the need for warehousing.

**Enhanced Digital Marketing:** With advancements in digital marketing tools and platforms, entrepreneurs can use targeted advertising, analytics, and social media engagement to reach and engage their target audience more effectively.

**Potential Challenges:**

**Market Saturation:** As more entrepreneurs recognize the benefits of self-publishing, the market may become saturated. Standing out and capturing reader attention will require excellent content, effective marketing strategies, and a strong personal brand.

**Quality Control:** With the ease of self-publishing, the challenge of maintaining high-quality content arises. Entrepreneurs must focus on professional editing and proofreading, cover design, and overall book production quality to compete and gain readers' trust.

**Distribution and Discoverability:** While online platforms like Amazon Kindle Direct Publishing have broadened access to self-published books, standing out among millions of titles remains a challenge. Entrepreneurs should focus on effective metadata and keyword optimization, strategic pricing, and proactive marketing efforts to improve discoverability.

The future of self-publishing for entrepreneurs is encouraging. By staying informed about emerging trends, leveraging technological advancements, and being aware of potential challenges, entrepreneurs can navigate the constantly evolving publishing landscape and seize opportunities to share their knowledge, grow their businesses, and connect with readers.

**Chapter Summary:**

The chapter discusses the increasing popularity of self-publishing as a powerful tool for entrepreneurs in the digital age.

It highlights how self-publishing provides creative control, rapid speed to market, increased profit share, and global reach.

The chapter explores strategies like aligning publishing goals with business objectives, choosing the right topic, developing writing techniques, using editing processes, and implementing marketing methods.

It provides tips for leveraging platforms, enhancing thought leadership, establishing credibility, and attracting new opportunities.

The chapter examines emerging trends like rise of e-books, diversity in content, personal branding, and technological advancements in AI, machine learning, and digital marketing. It also discusses potential challenges such as market saturation, quality control, and distribution.

Overall, the chapter emphasizes how self-publishing enables entrepreneurs to share knowledge, grow their business, and connect with readers in the evolving publishing landscape.

**In our next chapter...**

Stay tuned for our upcoming chapter where we delve deeper into the world of self-publishing! Discover how taking control of your content, style, and design can help you authentically represent your brand and expertise.

Learn how authorship can elevate your credibility, position you as a thought leader, and help you attract new clients. Understand the enhanced profit potential and cost-effectiveness of self-publishing versus traditional contracts and appreciate the speed and flexibility it offers.

Explore how a self-published book can boost customer engagement, provide long-term visibility, and build your brand.

Get ready to dive into revenue diversification with consulting services, speaking engagements, online courses, and more, all made possible by the credibility gained from authorship.

Don't miss our next chapter!

$\sim$

## CHAPTER TWO

# THE BENEFITS OF SELF-PUBLISHING IN BUSINESS GROWTH

**GREATER CONTROL & Ownership:**

By self-publishing, business professionals can exercise greater control and ownership over their book, enabling them to create a more authentic and personalized representation of their brand and expertise. This freedom extends to all parts of the book, including the content, style, and design.

Content is the foundation of any book, and self-publishing lets business professionals have complete control over what they include in their work. They can decide on the topics, ideas, and insights to be shared, making sure the content aligns perfectly with their expertise and the message they want to convey. With traditional publishing, authors may have to change or compromise their content to fit the preferences of a publishing house. Self-publishing eliminates these limitations, letting authors present their ideas in an uncompromized and authentic manner.

In addition to content, self-publishing enables business professionals to exercise creative control over the style of their book. They can choose the tone, voice, and narrative style that best reflects their personality and brand image. This personal touch helps in establishing a stronger rapport with the readers, creating a more relatable and engaging reading experience. Traditional publishing often involves working with editors who may have different ideas on style, resulting in alterations that may dilute the author's unique voice. Self-publishing eliminates these variations and makes sure the book maintains the author's intended style.

The design of the book plays a crucial role in creating a visually appealing and cohesive presentation. With self-publishing, business professionals have the authority to decide on the book's cover design, interior layout, images, and other visual elements. This lets them align the book's aesthetics with their brand identity, creating a consistent and recognizable image across all their marketing efforts. Traditional publishing usually assigns the design to professionals who may have a limited understanding of the author's brand, potentially leading to a design that does not accurately represent their image. Self-publishing grants the author complete control over the visual representation of their book, ensuring it complements their personal and professional branding.

Greater control and ownership offered by self-publishing empower business professionals to create a book that reflects their true expertise, style, and brand identity. This leads to a more genuine and impactful representation of their skills, resonating with their audience on a deeper level and establishing them as credible thought leaders in their respective fields.

**Increased Credibility and Authority:**

Self-publishing a book can significantly boost a business owner's credibility and authority within their industry or niche. The act of publishing a book alone has an air of expertise and leadership, positioning the individual as someone who has in-depth knowledge and insights.

When a business owner self-publishes a book, it shows a commitment to their craft and a willingness to share their expertise with the wider community. This act alone sets them apart from their competitors, as it showcases a genuine passion for their field of work and a desire to contribute to its growth and development.

A published book acts as a powerful marketing tool, helping to attract new clients and customers. When potential clients see that a business owner has taken the time and effort to write and publish a book, they perceive them as someone who has a wealth of knowledge and experience. This perception instills confidence in the individual's ability to deliver high-quality products or services.

In addition to attracting new clients, publishing a book also lets business owners solidify their position as thought leaders in their industry. It provides them with a platform to share their unique insights, ideas, and perspectives. As readers engage with the book and find value in its content, the author gains recognition as an authority figure within their field.

Having a published book also opens doors to speaking engagements, media appearances, and other opportunities to expand one's reach and influence. Being an author adds credibility to the business owner's bio or resume, making them more likely to be seen as an expert within their industry.

A self-published book offers the freedom to convey ideas and knowledge without constraints imposed by traditional publishers. It lets business owners write authentically, catering specifically to their target audience's needs and interests. This authenticity further enhances the perception of expertise and genuine leadership.

Self-publishing a book is an effective way for business owners to increase their credibility and authority within their industry or niche. It positions them as thought leaders and experts, attracting new clients and solidifying their reputation. By sharing their knowledge and insights through a book, business owners can establish themselves as leaders in their field and open doors to new opportunities for growth and success.

· · ·

**Case Study: John Davis - The Plumber Who Wrote the Book on DIY Home Repairs** (This story is a fictional example for illustrative purposes)

John Davis has been a plumber for over 15 years, running a modest local plumbing business. Despite quality work, John struggled to attract enough clients to exceed $70,000 in annual revenue.

In 2021, John wrote a book sharing his insights and tips for common household repairs. He wanted to establish his expertise and get home-owners to fix minor issues themselves. The book was titled "The Weekend Plumber: Basic DIY Repairs to Save You Money."

John self-published both e-book and printed versions of the book. He gave away free copies to new email subscribers and promoted it heavily on neighborhood Facebook groups. Local hardware stores agreed to stock the book after securing wholesale bulk orders.

Within a year, John had sold over 3,000 copies of the book. He was being called upon for local news interviews about DIY home projects. Many readers contacted John for major plumbing jobs they felt exceeded their abilities.

John's plumbing business grew to over $250,000 in annual revenue as he positioned himself as an affordable plumber and knowledgeable home repair adviser through his book. By sharing his expertise, the book let John build community recognition and trust to grow his local business.

**John shares his writing and self-publishing journey:**

Writing The Weekend Plumber was a gamble that really paid off for my business. As a veteran plumber, I had collected years of knowledge fixing common leaks, clogs, and other household issues. But I was struggling to attract enough clients to keep growing.

I realized that if I could position myself as the helpful neighborhood plumber by sharing DIY tips, it would build trust and recognition for my services. By teaching people basic repairs through my book, I hoped to empower them while also showing my expertise.

Writing the book forced me to explain repairs step-by-step in everyday terms. Promoting it locally let me give back to my community. I never expected it to take off the way it did. Soon I was being interviewed by local media and hardware stores couldn't keep the book in stock.

Most important, the book delivered results for my business. Readers who tried repairs themselves but found them too difficult contacted me. They saw me as an authoritative but accessible plumber they could trust. My revenue increased over 3X within a year as the book helped drive referrals.

While writing the book required significant effort, it was one of the best investments I've made in my business. By generously sharing my knowledge rather than guarding trade secrets, I established myself as a neighborhood plumber who cares about helping homeowners. The book became a lead generator and credibility builder. My gamble showed providing free value to build trust will pay dividends. I'm so glad I stepped out of my comfort zone to try something new. Self-publishing The Weekend Plumber was a defining decision that let me grow my business to the next level.

**Profit Potential and Cost-Effectiveness:**

Self-publishing allows authors to unlock significant profit potential and achieve a high level of cost-effectiveness compared to traditional publishing contracts. One of the main advantages of self-publishing is that authors keep much of the book profits. In the traditional publishing model, authors typically receive only a small percentage of the sales revenue, with the majority going to the publisher and other intermediaries involved.

By self-publishing, authors have the freedom to set their own pricing and royalty rates, letting them maximize their earnings. With complete control over pricing, authors can experiment with different strategies to find the sweet spot that balances affordability for readers while still generating significant revenue.

Self-publishing eliminates the need for agents or middlemen, further reducing costs for authors. Traditional publishing often requires authors to work with literary agents who take a percentage of the profits as their commission. By bypassing this step, self-published authors can keep the full earnings from their books, enhancing their overall profit potential.

Additionally, self-publishing platforms and services have become increasingly accessible and affordable. Many e-book publishing platforms, such as Amazon Kindle Direct Publishing (KDP) or Smashwords, offer free or low-cost publishing options, letting authors invest a smaller amount upfront. This cost-effectiveness extends to print-on-demand services, where authors only pay for printed copies as they are sold, eliminating the need for expensive inventory storage.

Self-publishing provides authors with more flexibility in terms of marketing and promotion. While traditionally published authors rely heavily on the publisher's marketing efforts, self-published authors can use various cost-effective strategies to reach their target audience. This could include using social media platforms, building author websites, engaging in content marketing, or participating in online communities and forums.

However, note that self-publishing success is not guaranteed. Achieving significant financial gain as a self-published author requires high-quality content, effective marketing, and a well-executed publishing strategy. Authors must be ready to invest time and effort into creating compelling books, building an author brand, and connecting with their readership.

Self-publishing offers a profitable pathway for authors, ensuring they can keep much of their book profits compared to traditional publishing contracts. By eliminating the need for agents or middlemen and leveraging affordable publishing platforms, authors can maximize their potential for financial gain. Still, self-published authors must be ready to invest in their books' quality and marketing efforts to fully exploit the profit potential and cost-effectiveness afforded by self-publishing.

**Flexibility And Speed Allowing for A Faster Turnaround and Responsiveness to Market Demands:**

Flexibility and speed are major advantages of self-publishing compared to traditional publishing methods. In the traditional publishing world, authors often face long waiting periods before their books are accepted by a publishing house or literary agent. Additionally, once a book is accepted, it may go through multiple rounds of revisions and edits, which can further delay the publication process.

However, with self-publishing, business professionals have the freedom to set their own timelines and release dates. They are in control of the entire publishing process, from idea to completion. This means they can work at their own pace and release their work to the market as quickly as they desire.

Self-publishing allows for a faster turnaround time, enabling authors to respond to market demands. If a particular topic or genre is trending, self-published authors can capitalize on this opportunity by quickly producing and releasing relevant content. They can adapt and change their work based on the ever-changing market landscape and reader preferences.

Self-publishing provides the flexibility to make edits and revisions without the need for extensive approval processes. Traditional publishers often have strict guidelines and established procedures for making changes, which can cause further delays. Self-published authors can easily update their work whenever they see fit, ensuring their books stay relevant and up-to-date.

The ability to set their own timelines, respond to market demands promptly, and make revisions without unnecessary delays gives self-published business professionals a distinct advantage in terms of flexibility and speed. They can adapt quickly to changing trends and meet reader expectations promptly, enhancing their chances of success in the competitive publishing industry.

## STRONGER CUSTOMER ENGAGEMENT:

In today's highly competitive business landscape, building strong customer engagement is crucial for the success of any company. One effective way to achieve this is by leveraging the power of self-published books. By writing and publishing a book that offers valuable insights and tips related to their industry, business owners can create a platform to engage with their target audience on a deeper level.

First, a self-published book allows business owners to showcase their expertise and establish themselves as thought leaders in their respective fields. By sharing their knowledge and experiences, authors can position themselves as trusted advisers, which attracts potential customers seeking advice and guidance. This positioning enhances the credibility of the business and creates a sense of trust among the audience, leading to stronger customer engagement.

A self-published book provides a unique opportunity to connect with the target audience in a more personal and meaningful way. By writing a book, business owners can address the pain points and challenges faced by their potential customers directly. This personalized approach helps to show empathy and understanding, fostering a stronger emotional connection with the readers. Customers will feel more inclined to engage with the business, seeking its products or services to address their specific needs.

A self-published book serves as a powerful marketing tool in today's digital age. By promoting the book through various channels such as social media platforms, websites, and email newsletters, business owners can effectively reach a wider audience. The book can be a lead generation tool, capturing the attention of potential customers interested in the topic. By providing value through the book, authors can convert these leads into loyal customers, driving business growth.

Additionally, a self-published book allows for ongoing customer engagement even after its first release. By encouraging readers to engage through comments, feedback, and discussions, authors can continue the conversation and build a community around their book and brand. This ongoing engagement not only creates brand loyalists but also attracts new customers, as satisfied readers are more likely to recommend the book and the associated business to their network.

A self-published book can be a powerful tool to strengthen customer engagement for businesses. By sharing valuable insights, establishing thought leadership, and fostering personal connections, authors can attract, engage, and keep customers. Using this unique marketing strategy, businesses can experience significant growth and success in today's competitive market.

**Long-Term Visibility and Brand Building Can Create Lasting and Impactful Impressions on Their Audience:**

A self-published book provides business owners with a unique opportunity to prove themselves to be experts in their field while building long-term visibility and brand recognition. Unlike other forms of marketing content that may lose relevance over time, a book can continue to drive brand awareness and exposure for years to come.

By strategically distributing their book through various channels such as online marketplaces, bookstores, and industry events, business owners can ensure their message reaches a wide audience over an extended period. This wide reach allows for the creation of lasting and impactful impressions on the target market.

A self-published book enables business owners to showcase their knowledge, expertise, and unique insights into their industry or niche. By diving deep into their subject matter, sharing valuable lessons, and offering practical advice, authors can position themselves as authoritative figures within their field. This elevated status builds trust and credibility among readers, ultimately strengthening their brand image.

As an added benefit, a self-published book serves as a powerful marketing tool that business owners can leverage across various platforms and media channels. It can be used to secure speaking engagements, media interviews, and guest blogging opportunities, further increasing exposure and establishing a strong brand presence.

Additionally, a book has a long shelf life, both physically and digitally. Traditional bookstores may continue stocking self-published titles for years, ensuring a continuous visibility that other marketing materials cannot achieve. Digital copies can be indefinitely available for purchase and download, letting potential customers discover and engage with the content.

A well-written and valuable self-published book also has the potential to garner positive reviews, testimonials, and recommendations that contribute to word-of-mouth marketing and extend the visibility far beyond the reach of traditional advertising methods. Positive feedback and endorsements can persuade new customers to trust and engage with the brand, boosting its reputation and increasing its customer base.

A self-published book offers business owners a powerful tool for long-term visibility and brand building. By distributing their book through various channels and establishing themselves as experts, business owners can create lasting and impactful impressions on their audience. The book's continued relevance and reach ensure that it generates brand awareness and exposure for years to come, ultimately contributing to the growth and success of the business.

**Diversification Of Revenue Streams Contributing to Overall Business Growth & Financial Stability:**

By self-publishing a book, business professionals have the chance to tap into various revenue streams and significantly broaden their sources of income. Apart from generating revenue from book sales, authors can capitalize on their knowledge and reputation to offer a range of services that contribute to their overall business growth and financial stability.

One way authors can maximize their revenue potential is by offering consulting services. Having authored a book positions, them as an authority in their field, making them valuable resources for businesses and individuals seeking guidance and advice. Business professionals can leverage their book as a credibility booster, attracting clients willing to pay for their specialized knowledge and experience. This consultancy service can be offered through one-on-one sessions, workshops, or even as part of a package deal with the book.

In addition to consulting, authors can also monetize their expertise by taking advantage of speaking engagements. Many organizations, conferences, and events are constantly seeking knowledgeable speakers who can provide valuable insights. Being a published author adds a level of prestige, increasing the chances of securing speaking opportunities. These speaking engagements not only offer monetary compensation but also offer exposure to a wider audience, potentially leading to new business opportunities and collaborations.

Another way to diversify revenue streams is by creating and selling online courses related to the book's subject matter. These courses can offer deeper insights, training, and practical knowledge beyond what is covered in the book. By leveraging their knowledge, authors can develop comprehensive courses that cater to different learning styles and cater to a larger audience. Online courses can be sold as stand-alone products or as part of a premium package that includes the book, consulting services, and more resources.

Authors can also explore other related products or services to further diversify their revenue streams. This could include developing supplementary materials such as workbooks, templates, or toolkits that enhance the book's content and deliver more value to readers. By creating these complementary products, authors can tap into new revenue streams while also strengthening their brand and expanding their reach.

Self-publishing a book opens up a multitude of opportunities for business professionals to diversify their income and expand their revenue streams. By leveraging their expertise, authors can offer consulting services, secure speaking engagements, develop online courses, and create other related products. These supplementary revenue streams not only contribute to financial stability but also foster overall business growth, letting authors maximize their potential and prove themselves to be thought leaders in their respective fields.

**Chapter Summary:**

The chapter discusses the benefits that self-publishing offers for business growth. It highlights how self-publishing provides greater control and ownership over content, style, and design, enabling a more authentic representation of the author's brand and expertise.

It explains how publishing a book increases credibility and authority, positioning the author as a thought leader and attracting new clients.

The chapter outlines the significant profit potential and cost-effectiveness of self-publishing compared to traditional publishing contracts. It emphasizes the flexibility and speed advantages of self-publishing, allowing for faster turnaround and responsiveness to market demands.

The chapter explores how self-published books can enable stronger customer engagement by showcasing expertise, addressing pain points, and using digital promotion. It notes that self-published books offer long-term visibility and brand building through wide distribution and establishing domain authority.

Finally, the chapter discusses revenue stream diversification through consulting services, speaking engagements, online courses, and supplementary products made possible by the credibility gained from authorship.

The key benefits highlighted include control, authority, profitability, flexibility, customer engagement, brand building, and revenue diversification.

**In our next chapter...**

In the upcoming chapter, we'll delve deep into the art and science of choosing the perfect niche for your self-published book.

We'll guide you through understanding your target audience in depth —their demographics, interests, and preferences—to ensure your choice resonates with them.

You'll receive advice on how to leverage your expertise, passion, and unique insights in the selection process, along with the importance of comprehensive market research.

We'll explore ways to determine your book's unique selling proposition and how to capitalize on it within your chosen genre. We'll also discuss the crucial step of confirming your niche choice and the value of testing ideas on a small scale.

As we round up, you'll learn how to consider the long-term potential of your niche for a sustainable and successful self-publishing career.

This chapter holds the blueprint to find the best niche and genre for your work. Don't miss it!

CHAPTER THREE

# IDENTIFYING YOUR TARGET AUDIENCE AND PURPOSE FOR WRITING A BOOK - CHOOSING THE RIGHT NICHE AND GENRE FOR YOUR SELF-PUBLISHED BOOK

**UNDERSTAND Your Target Audience to Choose a Niche That Resonates with Them:**

Understanding your target audience is essential when developing content that resonates with them. By conducting thorough research and identifying their demographics, interests, and preferences, you can choose a niche that effectively engages your potential readers. Here are the steps to achieve this:

**Define your goals:** Before diving into audience research, clearly define your goals. Understand what you aim to achieve through your content and how it aligns with your overall strategy.

**Gather demographic information:** Start by collecting essential demographic data about your potential readers, such as age, gender, location, education level, income, and occupation. This information will help you outline a basic profile of your target audience.

**Conduct surveys and interviews:** To gain deeper insights, conduct surveys or interviews with your target audience. Ask questions about their interests, habits, challenges, and preferences. This qualitative data will provide valuable insights into their mindset and motivations.

**Analyze social media data:** Social media platforms offer plenty of information about user preferences. Analyze data from platforms like Facebook, Twitter, and Instagram to understand popular topics, trends, and online discussions relevant to your potential readers.

**Track online forums and communities:** Explore online forums, discussion boards, and communities related to your niche. Pay attention to the questions people ask, the issues they face, and the resources they seek. This will help you understand their pain points and what they find interesting.

**Use analytics tools:** Take advantage of analytics tools like Google Analytics, which provide comprehensive data about website visitors. Analyze metrics such as page views, average time spent on specific pages, and bounce rate to understand which topics or types of content attract more engagement.

**Analyze competitor strategies:** Study your competitors' content, websites, and social media presence. Identify the tactics they use to engage with your target audience and determine what works well for them. This analysis can provide insights for differentiating your own content.

**Create audience personas:** Based on the information gathered, create audience personas – fictional characters that represent different segments of your target audience. Include their demographics, interests, preferences, and pain points. This will help you create content that addresses their specific needs.

**Test and refine your niche:** Use the insights gained from your research to select a niche that aligns with your target audience's demographics, interests, and preferences. Create content in this niche and measure engagement metrics like clicks, shares, and comments. Based on the feedback, make changes and refine your niche as needed.

Remember that understanding your target audience is an ongoing process. Stay updated with current trends, preferences, and changes in demographics to ensure your content remains relevant and resonates with your readers.

**Evaluate Your Expertise and Passion:**

When evaluating your expertise and passion for a particular subject or genre, it is crucial to take an honest and introspective approach. Choosing a niche that aligns with your interests will not only keep you motivated but also let you produce high-quality content that resonates with your audience. Here are steps to evaluate and determine your expertise and passion:

**Identify your areas of knowledge:** Begin by listing the subjects or genres you have in-depth knowledge about. Consider your educational background, work experience, hobbies, or any other areas where you have collected knowledge. This could include anything from technology and fitness to fashion or travel.

**Assess your skills and experience:** Evaluate your skill in each of the identified areas. Determine your level of knowledge and the extent of your experience in those subjects. Consider your ability to teach or communicate about the topic effectively.

**Reflect on your passions and interests:** Next, analyze what excites and interests you. Think about what you enjoy doing in your free time, what topics you constantly read or learn about, or what conversations you engage in most passionately. These are indications of your genuine passions.

**Identify your unique perspective:** Consider what sets you apart from others in your chosen subject or genre. Reflect on your own life experiences, values, and viewpoints that can add a unique flavor to the content you create. This individuality will make your content more compelling and attract a specific audience.

**Research market demand:** Although passion is essential, it is also vital to evaluate the market demand for your chosen niche. Determine if there is an audience interested in and seeking content related to your subject or genre. This will ensure your efforts are not in vain and that your content will reach the intended audience.

**Review your motivation levels:** last, honestly assess your level of motivation and commitment toward your chosen niche. Evaluate if you can sustain enthusiasm and dedication in the long run. Remember, choosing a niche solely based on current trends may lead to burnout if you lack genuine passion.

By evaluating your knowledge and passion, you can select a niche that aligns with your interests and keeps you motivated to produce high-quality content. Remember, staying true to your genuine interests will not only enhance the value of your content but also help with your personal growth and fulfillment.

**Conduct Market Research for The Potential for Success and Profitability Before Deciding on A Specific Niche:**

Conducting market research is a crucial step before deciding on a specific niche or genre. It helps you understand the market demand, competition, and trends in various niches. This analysis lets you evaluate the potential for success and profitability, enabling you to make informed decisions about your business strategy.

Here are the steps to conduct thorough market research:

**Define the scope:** Determine the scope of your research, such as the industries or genres you want to explore. This could include technology, health and wellness, fashion, entertainment, food, or any other area of interest.

**Identify target audience:** Identify the target audience for your chosen niche. This entails understanding their demographics, preferences, behavior, and purchasing power. This information will help you tailor your product or service to meet their needs and preferences effectively.

**Analyze market demand:** Research the size and growth rate of the market for your chosen niche. Look for data on industry reports, market research firms, government databases, and trade associations. This will give you insights into the potential customer base and overall demand for your product or service.

**Study competition:** Analyze the competitors operating within your desired niche. Identify both direct and indirect competitors, understanding their strengths, weaknesses, market share, and pricing strategies. This analysis will help you identify gaps in the market that you can fill and differentiate yourself from existing players.

**Analyze trends:** Identify and analyze the latest trends and developments within your chosen niche. Keeping up with these trends will help you stay relevant in the market and adapt your offerings as consumer preferences change. Look for industry reports, trade publications, influential blogs, and social media platforms to gather relevant information.

**Evaluate profitability:** Assess the profitability potential of your chosen niche by looking at factors such as production costs, pricing strategies of competitors, market pricing, and potential revenue streams. This assessment will help you determine if your chosen niche is financially viable and if it aligns with your business goals.

**Gather consumer insights:** Conduct surveys, interviews, or focus groups to gather direct feedback from your target audience. Understanding consumer needs, pain points, and preferences will provide valuable insights for product development and marketing strategies.

**Track industry influencers:** Identify key influencers and thought leaders within your chosen niche. Follow their content, social media presence, and interactions with their audience. This will give you a deeper understanding of market dynamics and consumer sentiment.

**SWOT analysis:** Conduct a SWOT (Strengths, Weaknesses, Opportunities, and Threats) analysis to evaluate the overall landscape of your chosen niche. This analysis will help you gain a comprehensive understanding of the potential challenges and opportunities within your market.

By analyzing the market demand, competition, and trends in different niches and genres, you can make informed decisions on the best niche for your business. This research will enable you to position yourself effectively, capitalize on opportunities, and maximize your chances for success and profitability.

**Consider Your Unique Selling Proposition (USP):**

The unique selling proposition (USP) of my book lies in its innovative approach toward the chosen niche and the distinct value it adds to readers. Unlike other books in the genre, my book takes a fresh perspective by combining practical strategies with relatable story-telling, allowing readers to not only absorb valuable information but also experience genuine connection and inspiration.

First, my book stands out through its incorporation of practical strategies. It not only offers theoretical knowledge but also provides step-by-step action plans, interactive exercises, and thought-provoking prompts. By presenting readers with real tools and frameworks, they can immediately apply the ideas learned in their real lives and see positive changes. This part distinguishes my book from others that may simply provide theoretical ideas without guiding readers on how to start them effectively.

Second, my book captivates readers through relatable storytelling. Rather than presenting dry facts or academic ideas, it uses real-life stories and relatable experiences to bring the ideas to life. By sharing anecdotes and personal journeys, readers can relate to the challenges, triumphs, and lessons of the characters. This narrative approach fosters emotional connection and empathy, enabling readers to engage with the content on a deeper level and enhancing its impact.

Additionally, my book adds value to readers by offering not only theoretical knowledge and relatable stories but also practical wisdom. It delves into the nuances of the chosen niche and provides insights often overlooked by other books in the genre. By offering unique perspectives, alternative viewpoints, and innovative solutions, my book equips readers with information and strategies they may not have found before. This added value makes sure readers are receiving fresh, valuable content that expands their understanding and enriches their lives.

Ultimately, by combining practical strategies, relatable storytelling, and practical wisdom, my book delivers a unique and valuable reading experience. It sets itself apart from others in the genre by providing readers with actionable tools, emotional connection, and new insights.

The USP of my book lies in its ability to not only educate but also inspire, motivate, and empower readers to transform their lives positively.

**Gauge Reader Demand:**

**Conduct market research:** Start by identifying your target audience within the chosen niche. Use online tools, such as surveys or social media polls, to gather information about their preferences, interests, and challenges.

**Analyze competitor content:** Study your competitors' content strategy to understand what topics they cover, what type of content is popular, and how engaged their audience is. This will show you what already exists and help you find gaps to fill.

**Engage with your audience:** Interact with your potential readers through comments on your own content, social media platforms, or online forums dedicated to your niche. Ask questions, seek feedback, and encourage discussions to gain insights into their needs, wants, and pain points.

**Monitor trends and industry news:** Stay updated with the latest trends, news, and developments within your niche. This will help you understand what is currently relevant and what readers may look for. It can also give you ideas for new and engaging content.

**Use keyword research:** Conduct keyword research to identify popular search terms and phrases related to your niche. This will help you understand what readers are searching for and what topics are in demand. Tools like Google Keyword Planner or SEMrush can help with this process.

**Analyze website analytics:** Monitor your website analytics to gather data on which pages or articles are performing well. Look for patterns in terms of topics, formats, or headlines resonating with your audience. This data can guide your content creation decisions.

**Engage in conversations offline:** Go to relevant industry events, conferences, or meetups to connect with potential readers face-to-face.

These interactions can provide valuable insights into their needs and pain points that may not be clear online.

**Seek feedback and conduct surveys:** Ask your audience directly for feedback through surveys or polls. This can be done through email newsletters, social media, or even within the content itself. Ask open-ended questions and encourage honest responses to better grasp their needs and wants.

**Use social listening:** Monitor social media platforms and relevant hashtags to understand what conversations are happening within your niche. This will show you the current pain points and interests of your potential readers.

**Regularly review and adapt your strategy:** Keep track of the insights and data you gather and adjust your content strategy. Continually staying in tune with reader demand and adapting your content will help you maintain a dedicated audience.

**Validate Your Niche Choice to Ensure Your Niche Has Enough Demand:**

When validating your niche choice, seeking feedback from trusted individuals or potential readers is crucial. Their opinions and insights can provide valuable perspectives that can help you determine if your niche has enough demand. Here are steps you can take to validate your niche choice:

**Approach trusted individuals:** Reach out to trusted friends, family members, or mentors who can give you honest feedback. Share your niche ideas with them and ask for their opinions. These individuals should have your best interests at heart and be able to provide constructive criticism.

**Engage in online communities:** Join relevant online communities, forums, or social media groups where your target audience congregates. Introduce your niche idea and seek feedback from the community members. Engaging with these individuals will give you valuable insights and let you gauge the level of interest in your niche.

**Conduct surveys:** Create a simple survey using online tools like Google Forms or SurveyMonkey. Design questions that can help you understand whether your niche idea resonates with potential readers. Share the survey with your target audience via social media, email, or online communities. Ensure the survey is concise and easy to complete, as this will encourage more participants to provide their feedback.

**Seek input from industry experts:** Reach out to established individuals or influencers in your chosen niche and ask for their opinion on your idea. These experts will know the niche, and their feedback can be invaluable.

**Research market trends and demand:** Conduct market research to understand the current trends and demand in your chosen niche. Look for statistics, data, and reports that indicate the size and growth of the niche. This research can help you determine if your niche has enough demand to sustain your endeavors.

**Test on a small scale:** Before committing to your niche choice, consider testing it on a smaller scale. Start by creating a blog, social media account, or a landing page to showcase your niche content. Measure the engagement, traffic, and feedback you receive during this test phase to evaluate the viability of your niche.

**Analyze competition:** Research and analyze the competition within your chosen niche. Examine their content, audience engagement, and overall success. If there are already well-established players in the niche, it may show that there is a demand. However, be ready to differentiate yourself and offer unique value to attract your own audience.

Remember, the goal is to gather as much feedback and insights as possible to make sure your niche choice has enough demand. Combine the opinions you receive with your own analysis, interests, and expertise to make an informed decision about pursuing your niche.

**Consider Long-Term Potential to Cultivate a Loyal Readership and Build a Sustainable Self-Publishing Career:**

When embarking on a self-publishing journey, it is crucial to consider the long-term potential of the niche and genre you choose to write in. By evaluating the sustainability and longevity of your chosen niche, you can make sure your work will not fade away as a passing trend but instead have enduring appeal. This foresight is essential if you aspire to cultivate a loyal readership and build a sustainable self-publishing career.

To assess the long-term potential of a niche and genre, several factors should be considered:

**Market Demand:** Examine whether there is a consistent and growing demand for books within your chosen niche. Are people seeking out and reading books in this genre? Research trends, reader preferences, and sales figures to gain an understanding of the current and future market demand. A niche with a dedicated and passionate fan base is more likely to have long-term potential.

**Tread Carefully with Fads:** Be cautious when considering a niche that is trendy. Some genres experience sudden surges in popularity but quickly lose momentum. While it may be tempting to ride the wave of a passing trend, this is not a reliable strategy for long-term success. Make sure your chosen niche has a strong foundation, established readership, and potential to endure beyond its current fad phase.

**Evergreen Appeal:** Look for genres that have timeless elements and themes. Stories that resonate with human emotions, universal experiences, and fundamental parts of the human condition have enduring appeal. Genres like romance, mystery, science fiction, and fantasy have stood the test of time because they tap into these universal themes. Seek niches within these genres that enable you to put your unique spin on timeless storytelling.

**Hone Your Expertise:** Consider whether you have the passion and enthusiasm to continually explore and contribute to your chosen niche and genre. Building a sustainable self-publishing career requires a genuine interest in the topic. Readers can sense when an author is genuinely knowledgeable and passionate about their niche, and this authenticity contributes to building a loyal readership.

**Diversify and Adapt:** Even if you choose a niche with long-term potential, it's essential to diversify your writing and adapt to changing reader preferences. The publishing industry is dynamic, with new trends and subgenres often emerging. While staying true to your niche, be open to exploring related topics or experimenting within the genre to keep your work fresh and engaging for your readers.

By carefully considering the long-term potential of your chosen niche and genre, you can make informed decisions that strengthen your self-publishing career. Remember, cultivating a loyal readership takes time and effort, but by staying true to your passion, continuously improving your craft, and adapting with the changing landscape, you can build a sustainable and fulfilling career as a self-published author.

**Case Study: Sarah Brown - The Accountant Who Wrote the Book on DIY Taxes** (This story is a fictional example for illustrative purposes)

Sarah Brown is a certified accountant who has prepared taxes for local clients for over 10 years. Despite having a solid client base, her annual revenue was stagnant at around $85,000.

In 2022, Sarah decided to self-publish a book titled "Do-It-Yourself Taxes: A Beginner's Guide to Preparing Your Annual Returns." Her goal was to establish expertise while empowering people to handle simple tax filings themselves.

Sarah self-published print and e-book versions and offered free copies in exchange for email sign-ups. She promoted the book on LinkedIn and accounting forums. Local libraries and colleges also ordered copies.

Within 8 months, Sarah had sold over 2,500 copies of her book. She was being interviewed by local media outlets as a tax expert. Many readers contacted Sarah for help on more complex tax issues beyond their abilities.

By positioning herself as an approachable tax adviser through her book, Sarah grew her client base by over 30%. Her annual revenue increased to over $110,000. The book let Sarah attract new business and reinforce her personal brand as a knowledgeable accountant.

～

**Sarah shares lessons learned:**

Writing Do-It-Yourself Taxes was a strategic move to grow my accounting business, but I underestimated how much I would get out of the process personally. As someone who loves numbers and details, writing a book seemed daunting at first. However, I discovered how much I enjoyed breaking down complex tax issues in simple, everyday terms that readers could grasp.

Promoting the book forced me to step outside technical circles and share my knowledge with a broader audience. Seeing the book resonate with people, with readers thanking me for demystifying taxes, was incredibly rewarding. Local media interviews gave me confidence and name recognition.

I'm proud to have created an accessible resource to empower people to handle basic tax filings themselves. By generously sharing my expertise, I was able to provide value to the community while also attracting ideal clients. Readers who needed help with complex returns came to me because they appreciated my clear, jargon-free approach in the book.

In the end, writing Do-It-Yourself Taxes delivered on my business goals and so much more. My revenue increased substantially as the book brought in new clients. But even more important, the process expanded my thinking. I discovered I loved teaching others and making tax ideas understandable. The book helped me find my voice.

Stepping out of my comfort zone to try something new - writing a book - was hugely gratifying personally and professionally. It let me share my passion while positioning myself as the approachable tax adviser for ideal clients. I'm so glad I pushed past my doubts and wrote Do-It-Yourself Taxes. The experience has enriched my career and life in ways I never expected.

**Chapter Summary:**

The chapter emphasizes understanding your target audience's demographics, interests, and preferences to choose a niche that resonates with them.

It advises evaluating your own expertise, passion, and unique perspective when selecting a niche. Conducting thorough market research to assess demand, competition, trends, and profitability is highlighted before deciding on a specific niche.

The chapter explains the importance of determining your book's USP and value add compared to others in the genre. It provides tips for gauging reader demand through market research, competitor analysis, engaging with your audience, and tracking trends.

Confirming your niche choice by seeking trusted feedback and testing ideas on a small scale is recommended.

Finally, the chapter stresses considering the long-term potential of your niche to cultivate a loyal readership and build a sustainable self-publishing career. Key factors include market demand, universal appeal, honing your expertise, and diversifying.

The chapter provides a step-by-step guide to strategically researching, confirming, and selecting the best niche and genre for your self-published book.

**In our next chapter...**

Coming up in our next chapter, we'll be diving headfirst into the nuances of defining your target audience with precision.

You'll gain insights into how a well-rounded understanding of demographics, interests, and needs can help you tailor your content to resonate deeply with your readers.

We'll walk you through the process of setting clear, measurable goals, using key performance indicators to align efforts seamlessly and evaluate your progress.

Discover the power of comprehensive research in anticipating your audience's queries and concerns and how an organized content calendar can streamline your workflow.

You'll learn how to match your writing style to audience expectations, building engagement, and trust along the way.

We'll guide you through the intricacies of optimizing content for search engines and how to use data analysis to continually refine your strategy for ideal results.

This chapter promises to provide you with practical guidance on creating an effective, high-performing content plan. Don't miss it!

## CHAPTER FOUR

# CRAFTING A COMPELLING BOOK CONCEPT THAT ALIGNS WITH YOUR BUSINESS GOALS

**DEFINING Your Target Audience to Tailor Your Content Specifically To Them:**

Defining your target audience is crucial in developing an effective writing and content strategy. By clearly understanding who your audience is, you can tailor your content to resonate with their preferences, needs, and interests. This not only helps you connect with your readers on a deeper level but also increases the likelihood of achieving your desired outcomes, such as generating brand awareness, driving sales, or increasing customer engagement.

To define your target audience, consider these factors:

**Demographics:** Start by examining the basic characteristics of your audience, such as age, gender, location, education level, occupation, and income. This information provides a foundation for understanding their general behaviors and preferences.

**Interests:** consider the hobbies, passions, and activities your target audience engages in. This gives you insight into what they like, what they spend their time on, and what topics or themes might captivate their attention.

**Needs:** Identify the problems, challenges, or aspirations your audience may have. Understanding their needs lets you create content that offers valuable solutions, guidance, or inspiration, positioning you as a reliable and trusted resource.

**Psychographics:** Look beyond the surface-level demographics and dive deeper into understanding your target audience's attitudes, beliefs, values, and motivations. This helps you craft content that aligns with their worldview and resonates emotionally.

**Communication preferences:** Explore how your audience prefers to consume content – whether it's through blog posts, social media, videos, podcasts, or email newsletters. Being aware of their preferred channels will enable you to choose the most effective mediums to reach and engage them.

**Existing customer data:** Leverage any data you have from earlier customer interactions, such as buying behavior, website analytics, or feedback. This data can provide valuable insights into who is already engaging with your brand and what content resonates with them.

By conducting thorough research and analysis, you can create buyer personas, fictional representations of your ideal customers or target audience segments. These personas help bring clarity to your content strategy, as you can better align your messaging, tone, style, and delivery to cater to their specific needs and interests.

Remember, your target audience may evolve over time, so it's vital to regularly reassess and refine your audience definition as you gather new data and insights. By continuously staying in touch with your audience, listening to their feedback, and tracking industry trends, you can adapt your content strategy to ensure it remains effective and relevant.

**Setting Clear Goals and Objectives:**

Setting clear goals is essential when developing an effective writing and content strategy. By defining what you want to achieve, you can align your efforts and resources toward meeting those specific goals.

Here are a few steps to help you establish clear goals for your content creation:

**Understand your target audience:** Before diving into goal setting, it's important to have a deep understanding of your target audience. Consider their demographics, interests, pain points, and preferences. This knowledge will guide you in creating relevant and engaging content that resonates with your audience.

**Identify key performance indicators (KPIs):** Determine the metrics that will indicate success in meeting your goals. For example, if your goal is to increase website traffic, your KPI could be the number of unique visitors or page views. If generating leads is your goal, track the number of conversions or downloads.

**Set specific and measurable goals:** Once you have identified your KPIs, set specific goals that are measurable. For example, instead of aiming to "increase website traffic," set a goal to "increase unique website visitors by 20% in the next three months." These specific goals help you track your progress and determine the success of your content strategy.

**Make your goals attainable and realistic:** While it's crucial to set ambitious goals, ensure they are also attainable and realistic. Setting unattainable goals can quickly demotivate you and your team. Consider your available resources, time, and any constraints, and set goals that challenge you without being overwhelming.

**Establish a timeline:** Define a clear timeline for meeting your goals. By setting deadlines or milestones, you create a sense of urgency and accountability. These timeframes will help you stay focused, evaluate progress, and adjust strategies if necessary.

**Regularly evaluate and reassess:** As you work toward your goals, regularly review and evaluate your progress. Use analytics tools and data to measure your performance against the established KPIs. By analyzing the results, you can identify what's working and what needs change. Be open to adapting your content strategy as needed to optimize your chances of meeting your goals.

Remember, setting clear goals is not a one-time activity. It is an ongoing process that should be regularly reassessed and adjusted based on your evolving business needs, industry trends, and audience preferences. By consistently tracking your goals and measuring success, you can refine your content strategy over time and continue to drive meaningful results.

**Conducting Thorough Research and Anticipate Your Audience's Questions and Concerns:**

Conducting thorough research is a crucial step to ensuring the quality and credibility of your writing. It provides you with accurate information, lets you identify current trends, and helps you expect your audience's questions and concerns.

Start by selecting reliable sources for your research. Use reputable books, scholarly articles, government websites, and journals to gather information. Make sure the sources you choose are current and up to date, as outdated information might mislead your readers.

Next, create a research plan or outline to guide your exploration. Define the key areas or topics you need to cover and create a timeline to allocate enough time for research and analysis. This will help you stay organized and ensure you cover all the aspects of your subject matter.

When conducting research, be thorough in your investigation. Explore different perspectives and various viewpoints to gain a comprehensive understanding of the topic. This will help you provide a balanced view in your writing, considering different opinions and arguments.

Additionally, note any current trends or developments related to your topic. This will let you incorporate the most recent and relevant information into your writing. Pay attention to changes in regulations, emerging technologies, or any other developments that may influence your subject matter.

While researching, keep your audience in mind. Expect the questions and concerns they may have and ensure your research addresses them. This will not only make your writing more relevant but also help establish your credibility and knowledge in the eyes of your readers.

Last, cite your sources properly. Correct and comprehensive referencing is vital to maintaining the integrity of your work. Use citation styles such as APA, MLA, or Chicago to give credit to the original authors and avoid plagiarism.

Conducting thorough research before writing provides a solid foundation for your work. It helps you gather accurate information, identify current trends, and expect your audience's questions and concerns. By taking the time to conduct thorough research, you ensure the quality and credibility of your writing.

**Creating A Comprehensive Content Calendar to Ensure Consistent And Timely Content Delivery:**

Creating a comprehensive content calendar is essential for effective content management and to ensure consistent and timely delivery of content. By developing a content calendar, you can organize your content creation process, schedule topics, determine formats, and set deadlines for each piece of content.

Here are the steps to create a comprehensive content calendar:

**Identify your target audience:** Understand who your audience is and what type of content they would find valuable and engaging.

**Set specific goals:** Determine the goals you want to achieve with your content, whether it's brand awareness, lead generation, customer retention, or thought leadership.

**Plan your content frequency:** Decide how often you want to publish content. It could be daily, weekly, bi-weekly, or monthly, depending on your resources and audience preferences.

**Choose content formats:** Determine the types of content that will resonate with your audience. This could include blog posts, videos, podcasts, e-books, infographics, social media posts, or webinars.

**Brainstorm content topics:** Generate a list of relevant and valuable topics that align with your goals and audience interests. Consider current industry trends, frequently asked questions, or common pain points of your target audience.

**Focus on and organize topics:** Sort your topics based on their relevance, seasonality, relevance to upcoming events or product launches, or any other factors that may influence content creation.

**Assign deadlines:** Set realistic deadlines for each piece of content. Consider the time needed for research, content creation, editing, and publishing. Allot time for quality assurance as well.

**Create a content creation workflow:** Develop a step-by-step process that outlines who is responsible for each task, from ideation to creation, editing, reviewing, graphics or multimedia creation, and publishing. This ensures everyone involved in the content creation process is clear about their responsibilities and deadlines.

**Incorporate search engine optimization (SEO) optimization:** Integrate keyword research and search engine optimization (SEO) optimization into your content calendar. Identify relevant keywords for each topic and plan to incorporate them into your content for better search engine visibility and higher organic traffic.

**Share your content calendar:** Make sure everyone involved in content creation, including content creators, editors, and marketers, has access to the content calendar. This promotes collaboration and helps team members stay on track, enhancing content consistency and delivery.

**Track and adjust:** Regularly review your content calendar to evaluate what is working and what may need change. Monitor content performance metrics such as engagement, conversions, and traffic to determine the success of your content strategy.

By creating a comprehensive content calendar, you can effectively plan and execute your content creation efforts. This guarantees a consistent stream of high-quality content that meets your audience's needs and supports your overall marketing goals.

**Tailoring Your Writing Style to Resonate with Your Target Audience Will Help Build Engagement and Trust:**

When creating content, it is essential to tailor your writing style to match your brand voice and tone. This is because the way you communicate with your audience can significantly affect their engagement and trust in your brand.

One crucial aspect to consider is whether you want to adopt a casual, conversational tone or a formal, professional approach. The choice between these two styles should depend on your target audience and the image you want to portray.

If your audience is relatively young and prefers a more relaxed and informal communication style, a casual, conversational tone might be most appropriate. This tone can make your content feel more relatable and accessible, enhancing engagement. It lets you connect with your audience on a personal level, creating a friendly and approachable image for your brand.

But if your target audience consists of professionals or you operate in a formal industry, a more formal and professional approach could be more effective. This tone can help convey a sense of authority, knowledge, and reliability. It is important when dealing with complex or sensitive topics that require a serious and respectful tone.

Adapting your writing style to resonate with your audience is crucial for building engagement and trust. By understanding the preferences and expectations of your target audience, you can create content that speaks to them. This will make them more likely to connect with your brand and view you as a trusted source of information or products.

Consistency in your writing style is also important for establishing your brand voice. Whether you choose a casual or formal tone, it should be reflected consistently across all your content, including articles, blog posts, social media updates, and emails. This consistency will strengthen your brand identity and make your content more recognizable to your audience.

When creating content, consider your brand voice and tone. Adapt your writing style to resonate with your target audience, whether that's through a casual, conversational tone or a formal, professional approach. Building engagement and trust requires understanding your audience's preferences and consistently delivering content that aligns with their expectations.

**Optimizing For Search Engines:**

When optimizing for search engines, incorporating SEO techniques into your content is crucial. By starting these techniques, you can improve your website's visibility and rankings in search engine results pages (SERPs). Here are effective strategies to consider:

Conduct Keyword Research: Start by researching relevant keywords and phrases that users are likely to search for when looking for content related to your website. Use tools like Google Keyword Planner or SEMrush to identify high-ranking and low-competition keywords that align with your content.

**Optimize Headlines and Meta Descriptions:** Once you have your target keywords, incorporate them into your headlines (H1 tags) and meta descriptions. These elements provide search engines with a concise summary of your content and help users decide whether to click on your link. Optimize them by making them attractive, relevant, and engaging to increase click-through rates.

**Create Quality, Informative Content:** Producing high-quality content is essential for ranking well in search results. Make sure your articles, blog posts, or website pages provide valuable and accurate information that answers users' queries. Use your target keywords organically throughout your content, but avoid keyword stuffing, as it can negatively affect your rankings.

**Optimize URLs and Internal Linking:** Structure your website's URLs to be clear, concise, and relevant to the content. Incorporate your primary keyword making it easy for users and search engines to understand the page's focus. Additionally, use internal linking to connect related pages on your website. This improves user navigation and helps search engines understand your site's structure.

**Improve Page Loading Speed:** Slow-loading pages can negatively affect user experience and search engine rankings. Optimize your website's performance by compressing images, minifying CSS and JavaScript files, and leveraging browser caching techniques. Speeding up your site enhances user satisfaction and search engine crawling efficiency.

**Mobile-Friendly Design:** With an increasing number of searches occurring on mobile devices, having a responsive and mobile-friendly website is crucial. Ensure your website is optimized for different screen sizes, loads quickly on mobile devices, and offers a user-friendly experience.

**Use Social Media Signals:** Engage with your audience through social media platforms and encourage them to share your content. Likes, shares, and comments on social media contribute to your website's visibility and credibility, potentially boosting your search engine rankings.

**Build High-Quality Backlinks:** Acquiring backlinks from reputable and relevant websites can significantly affect your search engine rankings. Focus on building relationships, producing exceptional content, and contacting influential individuals or businesses in your industry for link-building opportunities.

Remember, effective SEO requires continuous tracking and improvement. Stay updated with search engine algorithm changes, analyze your website's performance using tools like Google Analytics, and make necessary changes to optimize your content for better search engine rankings.

**Analyzing And Refining Your Strategy to Achieve Better Results Over Time:**

Analyzing and refining your strategy is essential to make sure your content strategy is effective and aligns with your goals. By regularly reviewing the performance of your strategy using metrics like website traffic, engagement, and conversion rates, you can make informed decisions on what is working well and areas that need improvement. This process lets you refine your strategy and achieve better results. Here is a step-by-step guide on how to analyze and refine your content strategy:

**Set clear goals:** Before analyzing your strategy, establish clear goals you want to achieve, whether it's increasing website traffic, enhancing engagement, or improving conversion rates. These goals will serve as a benchmark to measure your strategy's effectiveness.

**Metrics selection:** Determine which metrics are most relevant to measure the performance of your content strategy. Common metrics include website traffic (e.g., unique visitors, page views), engagement (e.g., time on page, social shares, comments), and conversion rates (e.g., lead generation, sales, newsletter sign-ups). Choose metrics that align with your goals and provide meaningful insights.

**Data collection:** Implement tracking tools like Google Analytics, social media analytics, or email marketing software to collect relevant data. Make sure all necessary tracking codes are correctly installed on your website and platforms to capture accurate data.

**Analyzing performance:** Regularly review your metrics to assess the performance of your content strategy. Look for trends, patterns, and comparisons to identify which content pieces, channels, or campaigns are performing well and driving the desired results. Quantitative metrics like website traffic can provide a general overview, while qualitative metrics like engagement and conversion rates provide deeper insights.

**Identify successes and areas for improvement:** Based on your analysis, identify what is working well and appreciate successful content or campaigns. Determine the factors contributing to their success, such as topics, formats, or promotion methods. Simultaneously, pinpoint areas that need improvement, such as underperforming content, platforms with low engagement, or ineffective promotion strategies.

**Refine your strategy:** Use the insights gained from the analysis to optimize your content strategy. Incorporate successful elements into future content, campaigns, or initiatives to leverage their impact. Experiment with different approaches to address areas for improvement. For example, if engagement is low on one platform, explore new content formats or adjust posting schedules to increase visibility and interaction.

**Test and measure:** After making refinements, test the updated elements to see if they produce the desired results. Track the metrics closely to assess the impact of these changes. If improvements occur, continue making the changes. If not, reassess and revise until you achieve the desired outcomes.

**Iterate and repeat:** Content strategies should be treated as an ongoing process. Continually assess and refine your strategy based on performance metrics and changing market trends. Regularly revisit your goals, track new metrics, and adjust your approach to ensure long-term success.

By regularly analyzing and refining your content strategy, you can maximize its effectiveness and consistently achieve better results. Embrace data-driven decision-making, adapt to market changes, and learn from both successes and failures to optimize your content strategy continually.

**Case Study: Mike Wilson - The Landscaper Who Wrote the Book on Curb Appeal** (This story is a fictional example for illustrative purposes)

Mike Wilson started his landscaping business 5 years ago and steadily built up his clientele through word-of-mouth. However, revenue growth had stagnated around $90,000 yearly.

Looking to expand, Mike wrote a book titled "The DIY Lawn Makeover: Landscaping Tips to Increase Your Home's Curb Appeal." His goal was to establish knowledge while empowering homeowners to do minor landscaping projects themselves.

Mike self-published the book and promoted it heavily on neighborhood forums and local home & garden Facebook groups. He offered free print copies in exchange for email sign-ups. Local hardware stores and nurseries also agreed to stock the book.

Within a year, Mike had sold over 4,000 copies of his book. He started securing interviews as a landscaping expert with local magazines and radio shows. Many readers hired Mike for bigger projects requiring expertise beyond what his book covered.

~

**Here's what Mike had to say on the matter:**

When I wrote The DIY Lawn Makeover, it represented a big step outside my comfort zone. As a hands-on landscaper, sitting down to write a book seemed daunting. However, I realized it was the perfect way to share my experience while providing free value to homeowners in my community.

Writing the book forced me to explain key landscaping concepts I often took for granted. Breaking down topics like proper planting techniques and maintenance schedules in simple terms required concentration I wasn't used to in my day-to-day work. However, the effort paid off tremendously.

Giving away free copies let me demonstrate my passion for both landscaping education and serving my neighborhood. The book provided helpful information, building goodwill and trust for potential clients. Promoting it led to exciting media opportunities that gave me confidence and credibility.

Most important, the book delivered results by driving new business. Readers who tried smaller DIY projects but then needed help with more complex landscaping hired me because of the knowledge I shared. My gamble to step outside my comfort zone as a writer let me position myself as the neighborhood expert.

Writing and self-publishing The DIY Lawn Makeover was one of the best moves I've made for my business. By generously providing free value, I was able to rapidly increase my reach and recognition. The book became a powerful lead generator while letting me give back. Though writing it took dedication, the effort empowered me to take my company to the next level. I can't wait to share my expertise with even more homeowners by writing a second book!

Through my book, I successfully positioned myself as a congenial landscaping mentor and my annual revenue skyrocketed by 40% to exceed $125,000. My book helped me in attracting fresh business and fortifying my brand image as a well-informed landscaper within the community.

**Chapter Summary:**

The chapter emphasizes defining your target audience, including demographics, interests, needs, and communication preferences. This enables tailored content that resonates with readers. Setting clear, measurable goals and key performance indicators is highlighted to align efforts and evaluate success.

Conducting thorough research provides accurate information and helps anticipate audience questions and concerns. A comprehensive content calendar is advised to organize topics, formats, deadlines, and workflows for consistent delivery.

Tailoring writing style, whether casual or formal, to match audience expectations builds engagement and trust. Optimizing content for search engines through keywords, quality content, technical factors, and backlinks is explained.

Finally, regularly analyzing performance data, identifying successes and improvement areas, testing changes, and iterating are recommended to refine your strategy and achieve better results.

The chapter provides practical guidance on researching your audience, setting goals, planning content, optimizing writing style, incorporating

SEO, and continually refining your strategy to create an effective and high-performing content plan.

**In our next chapter...**

In the upcoming chapter, we'll deep dive into the well-crafted art of creating persuasive titles and captivating book covers.

We'll explore the power of stirring emotions in readers through your titles and covers, and how it leads to an increase in sales potential.

You'll learn the significance of visuals on covers as an effective tool for marketing, and how it can affect your branding while encouraging sales.

We'll guide you through the intricate balance of creativity and clarity to attract the intended readership. The chapter also emphasizes the importance of research-oriented approaches, including market research, competitor analysis, and reader surveys, for optimizing your titles.

You'll see how leveraging nostalgia and familiarity can foster connections and increase interest among your readers.

Additionally, we'll delve into the psychology behind fonts, colors, and design elements, revealing how these aesthetic choices can emotionally resonate with your audience and influence their purchasing decisions.

This chapter is packed with practical guidance on driving engagement and sales by making strategic choices that attract readers. Don't miss it!

## CHAPTER FIVE

# CRAFTING COMPELLING BOOK TITLES AND EYE-CATCHING BOOK COVERS THAT DRIVE SALES & FORMATTING THE INTERIOR

**THE IMPORTANCE of a Captivating Title to Grab Readers' Attention and Generate Curiosity, Leading to Increased Sales:**

In the competitive world of book publishing, a captivating title is a powerful tool that can make or break a book's success. A well-crafted book title instantly grabs readers' attention and generates curiosity, ultimately leading to increased sales. Here, we will explore the significance of a captivating book title and how it influences readers' purchasing decisions.

First and foremost, a captivating title acts as the initial point of contact between a book and its potential readers. In a bookstore or online marketplace filled with numerous options, it is the title that stands out and demands attention. A title that is intriguing, thought-provoking, or even just cleverly worded, has the ability to entice readers to pick up the book, entangling them in a web of curiosity and intrigue.

A captivating book title not only grabs attention but also generates interest and compels readers to delve deeper into the contents of the book. When a title suggests a hint of mystery, poses an intriguing question, or promises something exciting and unique, readers are naturally inclined to explore further. A well-crafted title can create a sense of anticipation, making potential readers eager to uncover the secrets and stories hidden within the pages, ultimately leading to increased sales.

Moreover, a captivating title can effectively communicate the essence of a book, giving readers a glimpse into its themes, genres, or main ideas. A title that effectively captures and conveys the spirit of a book ensures that the right target audience is attracted. By crafting a title that aligns with the interests and preferences of potential readers, authors and publishers can maximize the chances of the book being noticed and purchased.

In the age of social media and online platforms, a captivating book title has the added advantage of being easily shareable. Readers are more likely to share and discuss a book with a catchy title, resulting in word-of-mouth promotion and increased sales. Furthermore, a captivating title can also improve the discoverability of a book in online search algorithms and recommendation algorithms, helping it reach a wider audience.

It is essential to note that a captivating title must not only entice readers but also accurately represent the content of the book. Misleading or irrelevant titles can lead to disappointed readers and negative reviews, ultimately hindering sales. Therefore, striking a balance between captivation and authenticity is crucial when crafting a title.

The importance of a captivating book title cannot be overstated. It is the gateway to capturing readers' attention, generating curiosity, and increasing sales. A well-crafted title acts as an invitation to explore the contents of a book, engaging potential readers on multiple levels. By understanding the significance of a captivating title and investing time and effort into creating one, authors and publishers can enhance the chances of their books standing out in a crowded market and capturing readers' hearts and minds.

**Unveiling The Power of Emotional Appeal: Creating Strong Connections Through Titles & Covers:**

In the fiercely competitive world of book publishing, authors and marketers are constantly seeking ways to captivate readers' attention and generate higher sales potential. While the content of a book plays a vital role, it is the emotional appeal that often determines whether readers will pick up a book or not. This section aims to discuss the significance of tapping into readers' emotions through compelling titles and captivating covers, as well as how these strategies can create a strong connection, spark interest, and increase the potential for book sales.

**The Importance of Emotional Appeal:**

**a. Understanding the readers' emotional landscape:** Readers are more likely to engage with a book that triggers their emotions. By targeting specific emotional triggers such as excitement, curiosity, fear, or nostalgia, authors and marketers can establish an immediate connection, building an emotional resonance that piques readers' interest.

**b. Evoking relatable experiences:** Effective titles and covers have the power to evoke readers' personal experiences and emotions, making the book feel relevant and relatable to their lives. This emotional resonance acts as a key driver, as readers are more inclined to explore content that aligns with their own emotions and experiences.

**Crafting Powerful Titles:**

**a. Creating curiosity and intrigue:** Titles that elicit curiosity and intrigue can be compelling enough to make readers pick up a book. By using emotionally charged language, enticing questions, or unexpected juxtapositions, authors can generate an immediate interest.

**b. Tapping into readers' desires and aspirations:** Titles that promise fulfillment of readers' desires or speak to their aspirations create a strong emotional connection. When readers feel that a book can provide them with the emotional satisfaction they seek, they are more likely to be drawn toward exploring its content.

**Designing Captivating Covers:**

**a. Visual appeal and emotional resonance:** Covers serve as the initial point of contact and play a crucial role in sparking readers' interest. By employing visually striking designs that resonate with the emotions and themes of the book, authors and publishers can create an instant connection and evoke curiosity.

**b. Conveying the mood and tone:** Covers that effectively convey the mood and tone of a book tap into readers' emotions, setting expectations and generating interest. For instance, a brooding cover might attract those seeking emotional depth, while a vibrant one might appeal to readers looking for a more uplifting experience.

**Increasing Sales Potential:**

**a. Generation of word-of-mouth marketing:** Emotionally appealing titles and covers not only attract readers, but they also increase the chances of readers recommending the book to others. This organic word-of-mouth marketing can significantly amplify the book's sales potential.

**b. Standing out in a crowded market:** With numerous book options available to readers, emotionally appealing titles and covers allow a book to stand out from the competition. By captivating potential readers' attention, the book gains a competitive advantage, leading to increased sales.

The power of emotional appeal in titles and covers cannot be understated. By tapping into readers' emotions, authors and marketers can forge strong connections, spark interest, and increase the potential for book sales. Crafting enticing titles and designing captivating covers not only attracts readers but also sets the stage for a compelling reading experience.

**The Role of Visuals in Book Covers: An Effective Marketing Tool:**

In the highly competitive world of book publishing, captivating visuals on book covers hold immense significance. Often judged at first glance, book covers play a vital role in attracting readers and driving sales. In this section, we will explore the importance of visually appealing book covers and how they function as a powerful marketing tool.

## I. The Psychology Behind Visual Appeal:

**A. First Impressions:** Humans are visual creatures, and our brains are naturally drawn to visually striking images. A well-designed book cover grabs attention and creates a positive first impression.

**B. Emotional Connection:** Visuals evoke emotions and can communicate the tone, genre, or theme of a book. The right combination of colors, fonts, and images can elicit an emotional response, enticing readers to explore further.

## II. Attracting the Target Audience:

**A. Genre-Specific Design:** A book cover should effectively convey the genre to attract the right audience. An appropriate design will signal to potential readers that the book aligns with their interests and preferences.

**B. Cultural Relevance:** Book covers need to be culturally relevant to resonate with the target audience. Understanding cultural nuances helps designers choose visuals that appeal to readers from different backgrounds and regions.

## III. Stand Out on Shelves and Online Platforms:

**A. Shelf Presence:** Visual appeal is crucial for a book cover to stand out in a crowded bookstore. A well-crafted cover grabs attention, even from a distance, enticing readers to pick up the book and delve into its pages.

**B. Online Visibility:** In the digital age, book covers serve as thumbnail-sized marketing tools on websites and e-commerce platforms. A visually stunning cover can capture online users' attention, prompting them to click, read the synopsis, and potentially make a purchase.

· · ·

## IV. Branding and Recognition:

**A. Author Identification:** Consistent visual elements on book covers help establish a recognizable author brand. A distinct visual identity can build trust and attract loyal readers to subsequent publications.

**B. Series Cohesion:** For book series, cohesive visual themes across covers create a strong brand that is easily distinguishable. The cover design should entice readers by suggesting a connected narrative and encouraging them to collect the entire series.

## V. Encouraging Sales and Longevity:

**A. Word of Mouth:** An eye-catching book cover might spark conversations among readers and generate organic word-of-mouth promotion. This can contribute to increased sales and long-term success.

**B. Merchandising Opportunities:** With visually appealing covers, books have the potential to go beyond traditional reading and inspire merchandise, such as posters or collectible editions. This further expands the marketing potential of a book cover.

Visually appealing book covers are a powerful marketing tool that entices readers to pick up a book and drives sales. By addressing the psychology behind visual appeal, targeting the right audience, standing out on shelves or online, establishing author branding, and generating word-of-mouth promotion, book covers play a crucial role in the success of a book. Thus, publishers and authors should invest time and effort into creating visually stunning covers that captivate potential readers and leave a lasting impression.

## The Art of Balancing Creativity and Clarity To Attract The Intended Readership:

The art of balancing creativity and clarity is a crucial skill for any author or publisher. In a world filled with countless books vying for attention, it becomes imperative to strike the perfect balance between unique, attention-grabbing titles and covers, while still conveying the essence and genre of the book to attract the intended readership.

Creativity is an essential aspect of book marketing. A thought-provoking and original title can pique readers' curiosity, enticing them to pick up the book and delve into its pages. Similarly, an intriguing cover design has the power to captivate potential readers, drawing them in to explore the story within. These creative elements serve as invitations to readers, making them curious about the content and encouraging them to take a chance on something new.

However, while creativity is important, clarity should not be sacrificed in the pursuit of uniqueness. A book's title and cover must clearly convey the genre, tone, and essence of the story to attract the appropriate readership. Without such clarity, potential readers may be misled or confused. For instance, a lighthearted romance novel presented with a dark and ominous cover might deter the intended audience from picking it up. On the other hand, an intriguing thriller with a cover and title that do not accurately represent the genre might fail to attract the right readership, leading to disappointment and negative reviews.

The key to achieving a balance between creativity and clarity lies in understanding one's target audience. Each genre has its own conventions and expectations that readers have become accustomed to. While it is important to stand out, it is equally important to honor these expectations to attract the right readership. By conducting research and studying successful books in the same genre, authors and publishers can gain insights into the kind of titles and cover designs that are proven to appeal to the intended audience.

Another way to strike a balance is to incorporate subtlety and symbolism into creative elements. A title can be imaginative while still hinting at the themes or atmosphere of the book. Similarly, a cover design can be visually stunning and unique, but include elements that provide subtle clues about the genre or storyline. This allows for creativity without sacrificing clarity.

Ultimately, the art of balancing creativity and clarity in book titles and covers is an exercise in understanding and connecting with readers. By crafting titles and covers that are attention-grabbing, unique, and yet convey the essence and genre of the book, authors and publishers can attract the intended readership and increase the chances of success in an increasingly competitive market. Mastering this balancing act can provide a significant advantage in capturing readers' attention and ensuring their journey through the pages of the book is as satisfying as promised.

## Research-Driven Approaches to Choosing Titles for Maximum Sales Potential:

Research-driven approaches to choosing titles for books can greatly impact their sales potential. By using strategies such as market research, competitor analysis, and reader surveys, authors can identify trending keywords and themes that can be incorporated into book titles. This section will outline each of these approaches and guide authors on utilizing them effectively.

### Market Research:

Market research involves studying the target audience and analyzing their preferences. Authors can use various techniques to collect information and gain insights into potential readers. This research includes:

**a. Demographic Analysis:** Understanding the age group, gender, geographic location, and interests of the target audience helps in titling the book appropriately. For example, a crime thriller targeting young adults may have a different title than a similar book targeting elderly readers.

**b. Social Media Analysis:** Monitoring social media platforms and online forums can help authors identify emerging trends and popular topics within their target audience. Utilizing social listening tools can provide valuable information on keywords or themes gaining traction.

**c. Keyword Research:** Using tools like Google Trends or keyword research platforms, authors can identify popular search terms related to their book's topic. Incorporating these keywords into the title can improve discoverability and increase the chances of the book being found by potential readers.

## 2. Competitor Analysis:

Analyzing competitors' titles is crucial as it helps authors avoid redundancy and gives insights into successful strategies employed by others in the same genre. The following steps can be undertaken:

**a. Study Bestsellers:** Analyzing the book titles of successful bestsellers in the same genre reveals patterns and themes that resonate well with readers. Identifying common keywords, writing styles, or narrative elements can guide authors in creating compelling titles.

**b. Differentiation:** While analyzing competitors, authors should also focus on areas where their book can stand out. Identifying gaps in themes or keywords that have not been fully exploited allows authors to create unique titles that attract attention.

## 3. Reader Surveys:

Directly engaging potential readers through surveys can provide valuable input for developing effective book titles. Authors can perform surveys through online platforms, social media, or mailing lists. Key considerations for conducting reader surveys are:

**a. Targeted Questions:** The survey questions should be designed to gather respondents' preferences in terms of titles, themes, or keywords. For example, authors can present multiple title options and ask readers to vote on their favorite or provide feedback on potential improvements.

**b. Incentives:** Offering incentives like discounted book pre-orders or exclusive content can encourage readers to participate in the survey, increasing the response rate and engagement.

**c. Experimentation:** Authors can also include alternative versions of potential titles within the survey to gauge audience response and preferences. This A/B testing approach provides insights into which titles have a higher potential for success.

By utilizing strategies like market research, competitor analysis, and reader surveys, authors can optimize their book titles for maximum sales potential. These research-driven approaches help identify trending keywords, themes, and preferences of the target audience, ensuring the titles resonate effectively and increase the discoverability and appeal of the book.

**Leveraging The Power of Nostalgia and Familiarity to Increase Interest in The Book & Drive Sales:**

In the ever-expanding world of the written word, capturing and maintaining readers' interest is a constant challenge for authors. One powerful tool that writers can employ to captivate their audience is the leverage of nostalgia and familiarity. By incorporating elements of nostalgia or drawing on familiar themes, authors can establish a connection with readers, evoking a comforting sense of familiarity that leads to increased interest in the book and ultimately drives sales.

Nostalgia, the longing for past experiences or a sentimental yearning for the way things used to be, holds a unique power over our emotions. It transports us to a different time, invoking memories, and eliciting a strong emotional response. When authors tap into this powerful feeling by incorporating nostalgic elements, they create a bond between themselves, their story, and the readers.

Drawing upon familiar themes has the ability to resonate deeply with readers and create an immediate connection. Whether it is exploring the timeless struggle of good versus evil, the power of friendship, or the triumph of love over adversity, familiar themes provide readers with a sense of comfort and relatability. These themes have a universal quality that spans generations, ensuring the readers feel a personal connection and loyalty to the story.

When readers encounter familiar elements or themes within a book, it sparks a sense of recognition and understanding. It triggers a surge of emotions, memories, and experiences, making readers feel as though they are revisiting something cherished from their past. This combination of nostalgia and familiarity cultivates a feeling of trust between the author and the reader; a shared understanding that the author understands their audience and wants to provide them with a gratifying reading experience.

This connection of familiarity also leads to increased interest and engagement in the book. Readers are more likely to invest their time and money in a story that promises to deliver an experience that aligns with their emotional needs. By creating a sense of nostalgia and tapping into familiar themes, authors demonstrate an understanding of their readers' desires, making the book more appealing and intriguing.

Furthermore, leveraging nostalgia and familiarity can significantly drive sales. Books that provide readers with a comforting sense of familiarity often generate positive word-of-mouth recommendations, leading to increased visibility and widespread popularity. Additionally, as readers become emotionally invested in the story and characters, they are more likely to seek out future works by the same author, establishing a loyal and dedicated fan base.

By incorporating elements of nostalgia or drawing on familiar themes, authors can create a deep connection with their readers. The power of nostalgia taps into readers' emotions and memories, while familiar themes provide a sense of relatability and comfort. This strong bond of familiarity leads to increased interest, engagement, and ultimately, drives sales. Through the skillful implementation of nostalgia and familiarity, authors can create enduring works that resonate with readers and keep them coming back for more.

**The Impact of Fonts, Colors, And Design Elements: Unveiling The Psychology Behind Book Cover Aesthetics:**

The book industry is an ever-growing market with intense competition for readers' attention. In this context, the right combination of fonts, colors, and design elements on book covers can significantly impact readers' perceptions and contribute to boosting sales. This section delves into the psychology behind font selection, color choices, and overall visual design, shedding light on how these elements effectively resonate with readers and drive purchasing decisions.

**The Psychology Behind Font Selection:**

Fonts play a crucial role in conveying the tone and genre of a book. Different font styles, such as serif, sans-serif, script, or decorative, evoke specific emotions and associations. For instance, serif fonts often project a traditional or formal feel, suitable for historical or academic works, while script fonts may elicit a sense of elegance or romance, fitting well with love stories or memoirs. By strategically selecting fonts that align with the book's content and target audience, publishers can capture readers' attention and establish an emotional connection from the very first glance.

**Color Choices and Emotional Resonance:**

Colors have the power to evoke emotions and influence readers' perceptions, making them essential in creating visually compelling book covers. Each color holds psychological associations that can impact readers' feelings and expectations. For example:

- **Red:** Symbolizes passion, evoking excitement, and energy. It is commonly used in covers targeted toward romance, thrillers, or action-packed novels.
- **Blue:** Signifies tranquility, trustworthiness, and reliability. It is frequently employed for covers in the self-help, memoir, or non-fiction genres.
- **Yellow:** Represents optimism, happiness, and creativity. It is often seen in covers targeted toward children's books or lighthearted stories.

By understanding the targeted emotional response, publishers can select colors that resonate with readers and visually communicate the essence of the book.

**Design Elements and Visual Appeal:**

Effective book cover design extends beyond fonts and colors; it incorporates essential design elements to enhance visual appeal and attract potential readers. These elements include layout, imagery, and symbolism. An aesthetically pleasing arrangement of elements can capture attention and convey the content's essence while enticing readers to explore the book further. Eye-catching imagery or symbolism can also create intrigue, generating curiosity and boosting the chances of potential readers becoming actual buyers.

**Boosting Sales Through Effective Cover Design:**

When fonts, colors, and design elements are meticulously combined, they contribute to a visually striking book cover that appeals to readers on subconscious and emotional levels. A cover that resonates with the target audience increases the likelihood of potential buyers clicking, picking up, or purchasing the book. Positive consumer response to an aesthetically pleasing cover enhances the book's visibility, drives word-of-mouth recommendations, and ultimately boosts sales.

The impact of fonts, colors, and design elements on book covers is far from arbitrary. By understanding the psychological nuances behind font selection, color choices, and visual design, publishers can strategically create covers that effectively resonate with readers, capturing their attention and influencing their purchasing decisions. A visually compelling book cover acts as a silent ambassador, inviting readers to dive into the world within its pages and contributing to increased book sales in a competitive market.

**Chapter Summary:**

The chapter emphasizes the importance of a captivating title that grabs attention and generates curiosity, leading to increased sales. It explores using emotional appeal in titles and covers to connect with readers, spark interest, and increase sales potential.

The significance of visuals on covers as an effective marketing tool is discussed, including psychology, branding, standing out, and encouraging sales. Balancing creativity and clarity in titles and covers to attract the intended readership is advised.

Research-driven approaches like market research, competitor analysis, and reader surveys are recommended to optimize titles. Leveraging nostalgia and familiarity to forge connections and increase interest is highlighted.

The psychology behind fonts, colors, and design elements is examined, noting how aesthetic choices resonate emotionally and influence purchasing decisions.

The chapter provides practical guidance on crafting compelling titles and covers through emotional appeal, visuals, balancing creativity and clarity, research, nostalgia, and design psychology. The overarching goal is driving engagement and sales by making strategic choices that attract readers.

**In our next chapter...**

In the upcoming chapter, we will delve deeper into the intricacies of self-publishing - a journey that moves beyond mere book writing.

We'll be sharing expert strategies on how to effectively use your book as a branding tool to prove yourself to be a leader in your field.

We'll walk you through the entire process, from selecting your unique niche, creating top-tier content, and impeccable editing to leveraging reviews and social proof.

More than that, we will explore how to create a robust online presence, collaborate with professionals, and actively participate in industry events.

This chapter will also underscore the importance of continuous learning to stay relevant in your field. Stay tuned to unlock these secrets and establish your authority with self-publishing!

~

CHAPTER SIX

# WRITING AND EDITING TIPS TO ENSURE A HIGH-QUALITY BOOK FOR MAXIMUM IMPACT

INTRODUCING **the Concept of Using an Outline or Storyboard to Structure a Book:**

Writing a book can be an exciting and fulfilling endeavor, but it can also be overwhelming and challenging. One of the most effective ways to tackle the writing process is by using an outline or storyboard to structure your book. Whether you are a seasoned author or a novice writer, using this technique can be immensely beneficial in organizing your thoughts, clarifying your ideas, and ensuring a coherent and engaging final product.

So, what is an outline or storyboard, and how can it help in structuring a book? Let's delve into these ideas:

**Outlining:**

An outline is a structured plan that serves as a roadmap for your book. It lets you create an organized framework before you start writing. The outline typically consists of main chapters, subtopics, and supporting points that will be covered in each section. It provides a bird's-eye view of your book's structure, helping you develop a logical flow and ensuring a smooth progression of ideas.

**Outlining Benefits:**

**Provides a clear organization:** An outline enables you to arrange your ideas in a coherent and logical order, preventing the book from feeling disjointed.

**Defines your scope:** By breaking down your book into sections and chapters, an outline helps you stay focused and maintain a consistent theme throughout.

**Highlights gaps and missing elements:** While creating an outline, you may notice areas where further research or information is required, letting you address those gaps early on.

**Improves efficiency:** With a well-structured outline, you can navigate through the writing process much more efficiently, saving time and avoiding unnecessary revisions.

**Section 1: Understanding the Purpose of the Book**

The purpose of a book plays a vital role in its creation, reception, and impact on readers. Clarifying the purpose of a book is important as it helps authors have a clear vision, maintain consistency throughout their work, and effectively communicate their intended message to the readers.

One of the primary reasons for determining the purpose of a book is to guide the author's writing process. Having a well-defined purpose helps to streamline the content, structure, and flow of the book. It lets authors decide on the relevant topics to include, establish a target audience, and choose an appropriate writing style. Without a clear purpose, the book may lack coherence and focus, resulting in confusion and disengagement for readers.

Another significant part of clarifying the purpose of a book is its impact on the readers' understanding and interpretation. When an author has a clear goal in mind, it becomes easier to present information and ideas in a coherent way. Readers benefit from this clarity as they can follow the author's arguments or storytelling without being overwhelmed or feeling lost. By understanding the purpose of the book, readers can engage with the material, extract relevant knowledge, and derive maximum value from their reading experience.

Additionally, the purpose of a book helps to establish the genre or category it falls into. A well-defined purpose enables authors to cater to the specific expectations of readers interested in that genre. For example, a non-fiction book to provide guidance and self-help advice can engage readers looking for practical solutions and personal development. But a novel with a purpose of escapism and entertainment can captivate readers seeking relaxation and imaginative storytelling. By clarifying the purpose, authors can effectively communicate with their desired audience and offer a more tailored reading experience.

The purpose of a book can also guide marketing efforts and influence how readers discover and choose their next reading material. A clear purpose allows publishers, booksellers, and reviewers to accurately categorize and promote the book, helping potential readers identify it as something they would be interested in. This makes sure the book reaches the target audience and increases the chances of it being read and appreciated by the intended readers.

Clarifying the purpose of a book is imperative. It guides authors in creating a well-structured and focused piece of work, helps readers understand and interpret the material, categorizes the book appropriately, and aids in marketing efforts. By defining the purpose, authors can make sure their book serves its intended goal, resonates with readers, and leaves a lasting impact.

## Section 2: The Power of Brainstorming: Unleashing Creative Potential

In today's fast-paced world, generating fresh and innovative ideas is a vital skill for problem-solving, decision-making, and overall success.

When faced with challenges or seeking new opportunities, brainstorming becomes a valuable tool to tap into the collective intelligence of a team or individual. It lets us explore diverse perspectives, think outside the box, and unlock a treasure trove of possibilities. In this section, we emphasize the need for brainstorming and explore various techniques that can maximize its effectiveness.

Foremost, brainstorming is essential because it stimulates creativity and fosters collaboration. By gathering a group of individuals with different backgrounds, experiences, and knowledge, brainstorming creates an environment that encourages the generation of unique and varied ideas. It instills a sense of collective ownership, where everyone feels valued and can freely contribute without fear of judgment or criticism. Through this collective effort, brainstorming enables us to unlock hidden potentials and explore uncharted territories.

To ensure effective brainstorming sessions, several techniques can be employed. One popular method is mind mapping, which involves visually organizing ideas around a central theme or problem. By starting with a central idea and branching out into related ideas and sub-ideas, mind mapping stimulates non-linear thinking and helps uncover connections that may have been overlooked. This technique not only helps with idea generation but also encourages a deeper understanding of the topic at hand.

Another technique that helps with effective brainstorming is free writing. This method involves writing down ideas as they flow with no constraints or judgment. By setting a time limit, individuals or teams can quickly jot down all relevant ideas that come to mind. Free writing removes the barriers of self-censorship and allows for the exploration of both conventional and unconventional ideas. This technique often leads to unexpected insights and breakthroughs.

While using different brainstorming techniques, it is crucial to encourage the capture of all ideas, no matter how far-fetched or seemingly irrelevant they may appear. In the initial stages, the focus should be on quantity rather than quality. By creating an atmosphere where every idea is valued and documented, individuals feel more comfortable expressing their thoughts freely. Even seemingly unrelated ideas can act as triggers or catalysts for further exploration, ultimately leading to innovative solutions.

Brainstorming is an iterative process. Effective sessions require both divergence, where a vast array of ideas is generated, and convergence, where ideas are refined and evaluated. It is essential to set aside time to review and evaluate the ideas generated during the brainstorming session. This evaluation helps identify the most promising ideas and develop actionable plans for implementation.

Brainstorming is a powerful tool that unlocks creative potential and helps generate fresh ideas in problem-solving and decision-making. By using techniques such as mind mapping and free writing, individuals and teams can explore diverse perspectives and tap into collective intelligence. It is crucial to foster an environment that values all ideas and ideas, no matter how unconventional or unrelated they may seem. So, embrace brainstorming, harness its power, and unleash your creative potential. The possibilities are limitless!

**Section 3: Creating the Outline**

We briefly mentioned *outlining* a few paragraphs back. We'll expand upon it next.

Creating an outline is an essential step in the writing process as it helps in organizing thoughts and ideas in a clear and structured manner. Creating an outline provides a roadmap for the writer, making sure all the main ideas, subtopics, and supporting details are organized effectively.

There are various methods of outlining that can be used depending on the topic and the writer's preference. One common method is the hierarchical outline, which follows a top-down approach. In this method, the main ideas are listed at the highest level, followed by subtopics, and then supporting details. This allows for a clear and logical flow of ideas, enabling the writer to see the overall structure of their work.

Another method is the chronological outline, which is useful when presenting information in a time-based sequence. This outline organizes ideas in the order they occurred or will occur, providing a timeline for the reader to follow. It can be useful in narratives or historical writing.

Despite the outlining method chosen, the outline helps in organizing main ideas, subtopics, and supporting details by providing a visual structure. It lets the writer see the relationship between ideas, ensuring a coherent flow of information. By segmenting the writing into main sections and subsections, the outline helps prevent the writer from going off-topic or including irrelevant details.

The outline acts as a reference point during the writing process, keeping the writer focused and on track. It serves as a reminder of the main points that need to be addressed and helps prevent important ideas from being overlooked.

Additionally, an outline helps in identifying any gaps in the writer's knowledge or research. By highlighting missing supporting details or weak connections between ideas, the outline prompts the writer to conduct more research or refine their arguments to ensure a well-supported and comprehensive piece of writing.

An outline brings structure and organization to the writer's thoughts and ideas. It helps in identifying the main ideas, subtopics, and supporting details, allowing for a clearer flow of information. Whether using a hierarchical or chronological approach, the outline acts as a roadmap, keeping the writer focused on the main points and ensuring a coherent and well-supported piece of writing.

### Section 4: Storyboarding Techniques

Storyboarding is a visual technique that is helpful for fiction writers or those looking to add a visual element to their book. Like outlining, storyboarding creates a roadmap for your book, but it uses images or sketches to represent the scenes or events that will occur. Each image comes with a brief description, helping you visualize the flow of the story, character development, and pacing.

**Storyboarding Benefits:**

**Enhances storytelling:** By visualizing your story, you can convey emotions, settings, and actions, creating a vivid and engaging experience for readers.

**Supports structural coherence:** Storyboarding visually represents how different scenes or chapters connect, helping you maintain a consistent narrative structure.

**Encourages creativity:** Working with images stimulates your imagination, allowing for unique and innovative storylines.

**Helps with collaboration:** Storyboards can be shared with editors, illustrators, or other collaborators, fostering communication and ensuring a shared vision for the book.

Whether you outline or storyboard, both methods offer valuable guidance during the writing process. They help you stay focused, maintain continuity, and produce a well-structured book that resonates with your readers. So, before you dive into writing, take the time to create an outline or storyboard and set yourself up for success.

**Section 5: Establishing A Clear Flow**

A clear and logical flow in writing is imperative for effective communication. It lets the reader easily follow and understand the ideas being presented, making the writing more engaging and persuasive. Here are reasons why a clear and logical flow is crucial in writing:

**Enhances comprehension:** When information is organized in a logical sequence, readers can grasp the main points and ideas more easily. They can follow the progression of thoughts and connect the dots, leading to a better understanding of the message being conveyed.

**Helps with retention:** A clear flow in writing helps readers remember the content more efficiently. If the information is presented in a way that builds on previous ideas, it creates a logical structure that aids in memory retention. A disorganized piece of writing may confuse the reader and make it harder for them to recall the information later.

**Increases readability:** Writing that flows smoothly is more enjoyable to read. It eliminates unnecessary digressions or abruptly jumping from one topic to another, providing a cohesive reading experience. A clear flow keeps the readers engaged and interested in the text, encouraging them to continue reading until the end.

**Establishes credibility:** A well-structured and logical flow in writing showcases the author's organization and thoughtfulness. It reflects professionalism and knowledge, increasing the author's credibility in the eyes of the reader. Conversely, if the flow is convoluted or disjointed, it can create doubt about the writer's competence and undermine the overall message.

**Aids in persuasion:** Whether the goal of the writing is to inform, persuade, or entertain, a clear and logical flow is essential. It helps the writer build a compelling case or argument, presenting evidence and ideas in a coherent way. A disorganized flow can weaken the writer's point, making it difficult for the reader to grasp the intended message.

**Saves time for the reader:** A clear flow in writing saves the reader's time. When ideas are logically organized, readers can quickly find the information they need, without having to search through a jumble of sentences. This improves efficiency and lets the reader extract the information with minimal effort.

A clear and logical flow in writing is crucial for effective communication. It enhances comprehension, aids in retention, increases readability, establishes credibility, aids in persuasion, and saves time for the reader. By organizing ideas in a coherent and logical manner, writers can effectively convey their message and ensure their writing has the desired impact on the reader.

**Section 6: Revising and Refining**

When creating a comprehensive outline or storyboard for any project, whether it's a story, presentation, or even a design, revising and refining is crucial. By iteratively improving your outline, you make sure your ideas are organized effectively and that your message or story flows seamlessly. Here's how you can highlight and approach this iterative process:

**Begin with a rough draft:** Start by jotting down your initial ideas and concepts without worrying about the structure or organization. This first draft is essential for brainstorming and lets you get your creative juices flowing.

**Evaluate and analyze:** Once you have your first draft laid out, step back and evaluate the overall structure and flow. Identify any gaps, inconsistencies, or weak points in your ideas. This evaluation process will help you gain clarity on what needs improvement and provide a roadmap for your revisions.

**Refine the organization:** Look at your outline or storyboard from a bird's-eye view and assess how the ideas and sections are connected. Ensure there is a logical progression and that each point builds on the previous one. Rearrange or restructure your outline to improve the flow and coherence.

**Offer seamless transitions:** Pay attention to the transitions between different sections and points. Smooth transitions prevent the reader or audience from feeling disoriented or confused. Use transitional phrases or techniques to connect ideas and guide the flow between sections.

**Seek feedback from beta readers or editors:** To gain an external perspective on your outline or storyboard, it's essential to seek feedback from others. Beta readers, colleagues, or editors can provide valuable insights into areas needing improvement. Listen to their suggestions and consider how they align with your first vision.

**Iterate and repeat:** Use the feedback received to iterate on your outline or storyboard. Make necessary revisions and improvements while keeping your overall goal or message intact. Remember, the iterative process may involve multiple rounds of revisions until you achieve a final version that meets your expectations.

**Tips For Reviewing and Improving the Organization of Ideas:**

- Use headings and subheadings to create clear sections and subsections within your outline or storyboard. This helps readers or viewers navigate through your content easily.
- Use bullet points or numbering for complex ideas or steps to enhance readability and comprehension.
- Check for coherence and consistency in the language, tone, and style used throughout your outline. Consistency makes your work more professional and easier to follow.
- Remove any redundant or repetitive information to keep your outline concise and focused.

**The Importance of Seeking Feedback from Beta Readers or Editors:**

**Fresh perspectives:** While you may be deeply involved in your project, feedback from others can provide new insights and ideas. They may spot issues you overlooked or suggest alternative approaches that enhance your work.

**Objective evaluation:** Beta readers and editors can offer a more objective assessment of your outline or storyboard, helping you identify areas that lack clarity or need further development.

**Quality assurance:** Collaborating with other professionals ensures your work meets industry or genre standards, enhancing its quality and marketability.

**Proofreading and grammar:** Editors can help you catch grammatical errors, typos, or other mistakes that might have slipped through during the iteration process.

The iterative process of revising and refining your outline or storyboard is essential for organizing your ideas effectively. Seek feedback from others, continuously evaluate and improve the organization, and remember that revisions may be necessary until you achieve a final version that meets your goals.

## Avoid Excessive Use of Adjectives & Adverbs: Show Don't Tell

Excessive use of adjectives and adverbs can weaken your writing and make it appear subjective or biased. Strive for concise and precise language that engages readers and effectively drives your point across.

Use vivid and descriptive language to create compelling imagery and evoke emotions in your readers. This technique lets your audience immerse themselves in the narrative and connect with your characters and story on a deeper level.

Lucy stood on the edge of the cliff, her heart pounding against her ribs like a trapped bird struggling to escape. Below her, the jagged rocks jutted out of the churning ocean, their icy spray biting at her skin. The wind whipped around her, tousling her hair and stinging her eyes with tears. She teetered on the precipice, the weight of her decision heavy in her chest.

A storm raged within Lucy's mind, dark clouds of doubt battling against beams of resolve. The memory of her father's disappointed expression haunted her, his disapproving words echoing through her thoughts. But a glimmer of rebellion flickered in her core, a spark of unyielding desire that urged her to defy the expectations that bound her.

With trembling hands, she unbuttoned her crisp white blouse and let it slip from her shoulders, revealing her bare skin to the ravages of nature. The icy wind licked at her exposed flesh, raising goosebumps that danced across her body like whispers of caution. The raw power of the elements wrapped around her, whispering in her ears and tugging at her soul.

Taking a deep breath, Lucy stepped forward onto the void. Fear and exhilaration mingled in her bloodstream, her pulse racing with a symphony of life. As gravity's grip tightened around her, she felt a surge of freedom that swallowed her doubts whole. For that fleeting moment, she defied gravity, defied expectations, and defied the suffocating weight of convention.

The ocean rushed up to meet her, its foaming jaws hungry and relentless. She plunged into the abyss of water, the shock of its chill knocking the air from her lungs. Darkness enveloped her senses, a world of muted sounds and swirling motion. Panic threatened to seize control as the pressure pressed against her eardrums, but a surge of liberation pulsed through her veins.

Arms and legs thrashing in the murky depths, Lucy fought against the current, each stroke a testament to her newfound freedom. With every kick, she shattered the chains that bound her to society's expectations, emerging from the watery depths like a phoenix reborn. The taste of salt lingered on her lips, mingling with the taste of victory.

As she emerged from the ocean's embrace, a triumphant smile spread across her face. The wind whipped through her soaked hair, a celebratory dance of liberation. The world around her seemed sharper, more vibrant, as if her plunge into the ocean had awakened something deep within her. The weight of the past and the burden of societal judgment had been washed away in the relentless waves.

Lucy gazed back at the cliff, the source of her transformation. It now stood as a monument to her courage and defiance, a testament to the power of choice. She would forever carry the memory of this leap, etching it into the fabric of her being. And whenever doubt threatened to creep back into her thoughts, she would remember the taste of salt, the rush of freedom, and the fierce determination that propelled her from fear to forever.

**Eliminate Unnecessary Repetition and Clichés from Your Writing:**

To enhance the quality of your writing, it is advised to remove any unnecessary repetition or clichés. These elements can divert readers' attention and render your work unoriginal or uninspiring. Instead, embrace creative and original expressions that enrich your book with depth and uniqueness.

**Proofread Diligently and Edit Your Work Multiple Times to Catch Any Errors or Inconsistencies**

Whether you are writing a professional document, a school assignment, or a personal piece, it is crucial to proofread and edit your work thoroughly. This process will help you catch any errors or inconsistencies and make sure your final product is polished and professional. Here are tips to help you through the proofreading and editing process:

**Take a Break:** Before you start proofreading, it is essential to take a break from your writing. This break will let you approach your work with fresh eyes, making it easier to spot any mistakes.

**Grammar, Spelling, and Punctuation:** Pay close attention to grammar, spelling, and punctuation. Incorrect usage of these elements can make your writing seem unprofessional and can distract the reader from your message. Use grammar-checking tools like Grammarly or the built-in spell-check in your word processor to catch any mistakes you might have missed.

**Consistency:** Check for consistency throughout your work. Make sure you are using the same tense, tone, and style throughout your writing. Inconsistencies can confuse readers and make your work seem disjointed.

**Read Aloud:** Reading your work aloud can be a helpful technique in catching errors. It lets you hear any awkward or unclear sentences that may need revision. Reading aloud also helps you identify if your writing flows smoothly, and helps you catch any missing or repeated words.

**Formatting:** Pay attention to formatting, especially if you are working on a document with specific guidelines. Consistent formatting can improve the readability and professionalism of your work.

**Seek Feedback:** Consider seeking the help of others during the editing process. A fresh set of eyes can catch errors you might have missed. Beta readers or professional editors can provide valuable feedback and help you refine your work even further.

**Proofread Multiple Times:** Proofread your work multiple times. After each round of editing, take a break and come back to it later. Each pass will let you spot different errors or inconsistencies that were overlooked.

Proofreading and editing are essential steps in producing a polished and professional piece of writing. By carefully reviewing your work for grammar, spelling, punctuation, consistency, and formatting, you can make sure your final product meets the highest standards. Please seek the help of grammar-checking tools, beta readers, or professional editors for an extra layer of scrutiny.

**Use Active Voice Whenever Possible:**

Active voice promotes clarity and directness, letting readers understand your message without confusion or ambiguity. Using an active voice can make your writing more engaging and livelier.

**Be Mindful of The Pacing of Your Book:**

The pacing of your book is a crucial element that can make or break the reading experience for your audience. It determines the rhythm and flow of the story, keeping readers engaged or driving them away. To ensure your book is well-paced, it's important to find the right balance between fast-paced and action-packed scenes, and moments of reflection or character development.

Fast-paced and action-packed scenes are gripping and exhilarating, grabbing readers' attention and keeping them on the edge of their seats. These scenes often involve intense physical or emotional conflict, high-stakes situations, or thrilling events. They drive the plot forward, create tension, and deliver an adrenaline rush to readers.

However, constantly bombarding readers with non-stop fast-paced scenes can become overwhelming and exhausting. It leaves little room for breathing, contemplation, or emotional connection with the characters. This is where moments of reflection or character development come into play.

During these moments, slow down the pace and let readers delve deeper into the minds and hearts of your characters. Explore their thoughts, feelings, motivations, and fears. Show their growth, their struggles, and their vulnerabilities. These introspective moments provide a necessary break from the high-octane action, letting readers develop a connection with the characters on a more personal level.

These slower-paced scenes provide an opportunity to explore the world-building, backstory, or thematic elements of your book. They let you create a more immersive reading experience by including descriptive passages and richly detailed environments, enhancing the overall depth of your story.

Remember, pacing is not just about balancing fast and slow scenes, but also about their placement and distribution throughout your book. Too many fast-paced scenes one after the other can lead to reader fatigue, while too many slow scenes in a row can cause the story to stagnate. Vary the pacing by strategically interweaving fast-paced moments with slower ones to maintain the readers' interest and prevent disengagement.

By finding the right blend of action-packed scenes and moments of reflection or character development, you can ensure a well-paced book that captivates readers from beginning to end. The careful balance of pacing will keep them hooked, eagerly expecting the next turn of the page, while a poor pacing may result in disengagement and loss of interest. So, be mindful of the pacing of your book, for it is one of the key ingredients that will make your story an enthralling journey for your readers.

**Leveraging Self-Published Books to Establish Authority and Expertise:**

Self-publishing a book has become increasingly popular in recent years to establish authority and knowledge in a particular field. By leveraging self-published books, individuals can position themselves as experts and gain recognition within their industry. Here are ways to effectively leverage self-published books to establish authority and knowledge:

**Choose a Niche:** Select a topic or niche you are knowledgeable and passionate about. This will give you a unique perspective and set you apart from others in your field. Focus on a specific area that will resonate with your target audience and highlight your knowledge.

**High-Quality Content:** Ensure that your book delivers high-quality content that is well-researched, informative, and relevant. Provide valuable insights, actionable advice, and case studies that showcase your knowledge. This will help establish your credibility and build trust with readers.

**Professional Design and Editing:** Invest in professional editing, proofreading, and book design to ensure a polished final product. A well-designed and error-free book will enhance your credibility and professionalism. It will also increase the likelihood of positive reviews and recommendations from readers.

**Leverage Social Proof:** Encourage readers to leave reviews and testimonials for your book on platforms like Amazon, Goodreads, or your website. Positive reviews and social proof can greatly influence potential readers and increase your authority. Consider reaching out to influencers or industry experts for endorsements or forewords.

**Content Marketing:** Leverage your book's content to create additional marketing materials. Repurpose sections of your book into blog posts, articles, videos, or podcasts. Share these on your website, social media platforms, or through guest posting on relevant websites. This will increase your online visibility, show your knowledge, and direct traffic back to your book.

**Speaking Engagements and Interviews:** Leverage your self-published book as a platform to secure speaking engagements, podcast interviews, or media appearances. Use your book's content for delivering insightful talks, participating in panel discussions, or sharing your knowledge with a wider audience. This will not only boost your authority but also expand your network and reach.

**Establish an Online Presence:** Create a strong online presence by building a professional website, maintaining an active blog, and engaging with your target audience on social media platforms. Consistently share valuable content related to your book's topic and engage in conversations with your audience. This will prove you to be an authority figure in your field and attract more readers to your book.

**Collaborate with Other Professionals:** Collaborating with other experts or industry professionals can help you expand your reach and establish your authority. Consider co-authoring a book, hosting joint webinars, or participating in collaborative projects. By associating yourself with other credible individuals in your field, you can enhance your own reputation.

**Go to Conferences and Events:** Go to industry conferences, seminars, and workshops related to your book's topic. Participate in panel discussions, deliver presentations, or engage in networking opportunities. This will not only let you share your expertise with a targeted audience but also establish connections and increase your visibility within your industry.

**Continuous Learning and Improvement:** To maintain your authority and knowledge, it is crucial to stay up-to-date with the latest developments in your field. Invest in continuous learning through books, courses, workshops, or certifications. Regularly update and improve your book's content to make sure it remains relevant and valuable to your audience.

By following these strategies, you can leverage your self-published book to establish authority and knowledge in your field. Remember, the key is to consistently provide high-quality content, engage with your audience, and actively promote your book and knowledge across various platforms.

**Chapter Summary:**

In this chapter, we explored the importance of pacing in storytelling and the strategies to leverage self-published books to establish authority and knowledge in a specific field.

We learned that the right mix of action-packed scenes and slower moments maintains a reader's interest throughout a book.

Regarding self-publishing, it serves as a tool for individuals to position themselves as experts.

Key tactics include choosing a unique niche, delivering high-quality content, investing in professional editing and design, leveraging social proof, content marketing, securing speaking engagements, establishing an online presence, collaborating with professionals, attending industry events, and committing to continuous learning.

These strategies can enhance an author's credibility, expand their reach, and establish their authority, all while directing traffic back to their book.

**In our next chapter...**

In the upcoming chapter, we explore the transformative power of self-publishing as a tool for authors to showcase their expertise and establish their authority.

We delve into the evolving landscape of publishing, highlighting how self-publishing offers authors greater control, autonomy, and opportunities to build their personal brand.

This chapter will provide insights into choosing the right niche, writing high-quality content, and building an effective author platform.

We share strategies to leverage reader reviews and expert testimonials to build trust and credibility.

You'll also learn how to secure speaking engagements and media appearances to expand your reach. We wrap up by addressing the value of collaborations, sharing ideas to connect with other authors and industry experts to enhance your visibility.

Don't miss this insightful chapter that outlines practical strategies to help you thrive in the exciting world of self-publishing.

## CHAPTER SEVEN

# THE RISE OF SELF-PUBLISHING - EMPOWERING AUTHORS TO BECOME AUTHORITIES

IN RECENT YEARS, the publishing industry has seen a significant transformation with the advent of self-publishing platforms. These platforms have revolutionized the way authors share their work with the world. Gone are the days when authors heavily relied on traditional publishing houses for recognition and authority in their respective fields. With the increasing popularity of self-publishing platforms, authors now have unparalleled opportunities to establish themselves as experts and authorities. This section delves into the growing prominence of self-publishing and highlights the empowering opportunities it provides for authors to become recognized figures in their fields.

**Evolving Publishing Landscape:**

The traditional publishing landscape was characterized by many gatekeepers and stringent submission requirements, making it arduous for aspiring authors to break through. This often led to talented authors being overlooked or dismissed. However, the emergence of self-publishing platforms has disrupted this status quo by providing an efficient and accessible alternative. Authors can now directly publish their work, bypassing the traditional barriers, and reach a global audience, despite the niche they cater to.

**Control and Autonomy:**

Self-publishing empowers authors by giving them complete control over their content. Unlike traditional publishers, who often have the final say in editing, design, marketing, and pricing, self-publishing platforms let authors make all critical decisions. They can keep their unique voice, maintain the integrity of their work, and independently publish at their own pace. This unprecedented freedom encourages authors to confidently prove themselves to be authorities in their respective fields.

**Building a Personal Brand:**

Self-publishing platforms offer authors a chance to construct a robust personal brand, which plays a pivotal role in establishing authority. As authors produce and distribute their work, they create a consistent presence that can extend beyond their books. With strategic marketing and branding efforts, authors can position themselves as thought leaders, generating a loyal following of readers who look to them for guidance and knowledge. Establishing a personal brand can help authors gain recognition, media coverage, and even speaking engagements, further solidifying their status as authorities.

**Expertise Validation:**

Self-published authors have the advantage of constantly showcasing their knowledge in their respective fields. Consistently producing quality content reinforces their authority and expertise in the eyes of readers. Additionally, self-publishing platforms help with reader engagement through reviews, ratings, and comments, enabling authors to directly interact with their audience. This direct feedback loop helps authors refine their work, enhance their credibility, and bolster their reputation as trusted authorities.

**Niche Domination:**

Traditional publishing often favors broad market appeal over niche knowledge. However, self-publishing platforms have revolutionized the industry by allowing authors to cater to niche audiences without worrying about commercial viability. Authors can now focus on highly specialized subjects and prove themselves to be go-to authorities in those areas. This niche domination not only increases an author's credibility but also opens doors to collaboration, speaking opportunities, and media exposure within their specific field.

As self-publishing platforms grow in popularity, they offer authors an unprecedented opportunity to establish themselves as authorities in their fields. With the ability to retain control, build personal brands, showcase expertise, and dominate niches, authors no longer rely solely on traditional publishers for recognition. By harnessing the power of self-publishing, authors can carve their own paths, gain authority, and shape their success.

**Choosing The Right Niche to Establish Authority & Expertise:**

**Choosing the right niche:** Exploring the importance of selecting a specific niche or topic to specialize in and how this can help leverage self-published books to establish authority and knowledge.

In today's highly competitive literary landscape, self-publishing has emerged as a significant avenue for aspiring authors to showcase their work and gain recognition. With the rise of technology and online platforms, writers can now reach a wider audience directly, without having to rely on traditional publishing houses. However, this increased accessibility has also led to a flood of content, making it crucial for self-published authors to differentiate themselves from the crowd. One effective way to do so is by choosing the right niche or topic to specialize in.

Selecting a specific niche lets authors focus their efforts and develop a deeper understanding of a particular subject. By honing their knowledge in a niche, authors can create a USP for their books. Readers, especially those passionate about specific topics, are often drawn to books that cater to their interests and provide valuable insights. By positioning themselves as authorities in a particular niche, self-published authors stand a better chance of capturing this targeted audience.

Establishing authority and knowledge through a specific niche also helps to build trust with readers. When authors show a deep understanding and wealth of knowledge on a specialized topic, readers perceive them as credible sources of information. This credibility lends itself to increased book sales and a loyal reader base. It can lead to collaborative opportunities, such as speaking engagements, guest blogging, or even consultancy work.

Selecting a niche also provides authors with the opportunity to create a brand identity. By consistently producing quality content within a particular niche, authors can develop a reputation as reliable sources of information and insights. This brand identity helps to establish a long-term relationship with readers, who will eagerly expect future releases and actively seek the author's work. Word of mouth within the niche community can further amplify an author's reputation and widen their reach.

In addition to the marketing benefits, focusing on a specific niche also streamlines the writing and publishing process. Research becomes more targeted and efficient, resulting in high-quality, well-informed content. This also enables authors to cultivate a loyal and engaged community of readers who appreciate their knowledge, encouraging them to leave positive reviews and provide valuable feedback.

Choosing the right niche, however, requires careful consideration. Authors should select a niche that aligns with their passions and knowledge, ensuring a genuine interest in the topic. Assess the potential market size and demand for the chosen niche, evaluating whether there is a significant audience willing to invest in books within that topic. Conducting thorough market research helps authors to understand the competition, identify gaps in the market, and tailor their content.

Choosing the right niche is paramount for self-published authors looking to establish authority and knowledge. By focusing on a specific topic, authors can position themselves as credible sources and connect with a targeted audience. Establishing authority within a niche builds trust, leading to increased book sales and collaborative opportunities.

A niche-focused approach streamlines the writing process and strengthens the author's brand identity. With the right niche, self-published authors can leverage their books to make a lasting impact and stand out in the competitive publishing industry.

**Writing Quality Content to Engage Readers and Build Credibility:**

In an age characterized by easy accessibility and abundance of information, it is essential for every writer or creator to generate top-notch content. Whether it be a blog post, an article, or a social media update, the significance of delivering content that showcases the author's knowledge, expertise, and unique perspective cannot be overstated. Not only does it capture the attention of readers, but it also builds credibility and establishes a strong connection with the audience.

One of the key reasons quality content is essential is that it engages readers. In an age where attention spans are dwindling, it is crucial to create content captivating and informative. By showing knowledge in a particular subject matter, the author instills confidence and piques the readers' interest. When readers find value in the content, they are more likely to invest their time and attention, resulting in increased engagement, such as likes, shares, comments, and click-throughs.

Publishing high-quality content allows authors to showcase their knowledge. A well-researched and thoughtful piece of content provides an opportunity for the author to delve deeper into a topic, present evidence-backed arguments, and share experiences or insights they have gained through their own unique perspective. By doing so, authors can position themselves as credible and authoritative voices within their respective fields. This builds trust and fosters a loyal readership who turns to the author for valuable and reliable information.

Additionally, delivering quality content contributes to building the author's credibility. When readers consistently encounter well-crafted and insightful content from an author, it establishes them as a trustworthy source of information. This boosts the author's professional reputation and opens doors to collaborations, partnerships, and opportunities for further growth. Credibility is a valuable asset that can not only attract new readers but also lead to increased visibility and recognition within relevant communities or industries.

Last, high-quality content enables authors to present their unique perspective. Each person has their own background, experiences, and way of thinking, which contributes to the richness of content creation. By sharing their unique insights, authors can offer readers a fresh and original perspective on a particular topic. This not only differentiates them from other creators but also fosters a sense of connection with readers who resonate with their viewpoint. This personal touch creates a bond that keeps readers coming back for more.

Producing high-quality content is imperative for any writer or creator. By emphasizing the author's knowledge and unique perspective, it engages readers, builds credibility, and fosters a loyal audience. In an over-saturated digital landscape, delivering content that stands out from the crowd is essential for success. So, every writer should strive to produce quality content that not only educates and informs but also creates an impactful and lasting impression on readers.

**Building An Author Platform to Connect with Readers and Establish a Loyal Following:**

Building an author platform is an essential step for aspiring or established authors to connect with readers and establish a loyal following. This platform enables authors to promote their work, build a brand, and engage with readers through various channels such as social media, blogs, websites, and other platforms. Here is an outline of the process involved in creating an author platform:

**Determine Your Target Audience:** Understanding your target audience is crucial when building an author platform. Identify the demographics, interests, and preferences of your potential readers. This will help you tailor your content, messaging, and communication style.

**Develop a Brand Identity:** To establish a cohesive and recognizable brand, determine your unique selling points as an author. Reflect on your writing style, genre, and themes, and use this information to create a consistent brand identity that resonates with your target audience.

**Social Media Presence:** Start by selecting social media platforms that align with your target audience, such as Facebook, Twitter, Instagram, or LinkedIn. Create dedicated author profiles and use them to share updates about your writing, engage in conversations, and promote your work. Interact with readers, respond to comments, and join relevant writing or book-related communities.

**Blogging:** Start a blog where you can share your writing, insights, and experiences. Regularly post valuable and engaging content related to your niche. This could include writing tips, book reviews, author interviews, or updates on your own projects. Encourage readers to subscribe, share, and comment on your blog posts to cultivate an active community.

**Author Website:** Establish an official author website where readers can find information about you and your work. Include an engaging bio, a list of published books, upcoming releases, and links to your social media profiles and blog. Provide a contact form for readers to contact you directly.

**Email Marketing:** Utilize email marketing to build a loyal following. Encourage readers to subscribe to your newsletter through your website or blog, offering exclusive content, updates, and sneak peeks. Regularly send newsletters to your subscribers to keep them engaged and informed about your writing journey.

**Engage with Readers:** Actively participate in discussions and conversations on social media, blog comments, and book-related forums. Respond to reader inquiries and reviews graciously and authentically. Show genuine interest in your readers' opinions and feedback.

**Collaborate with Influencers:** Collaborate with influencers, bloggers, or book reviewers in your genre to expand your reach and tap into their existing audience. Consider guest blogging, participating in author interviews, or offering book giveaways to build relationships with these influencers.

**Promote Your Work:** Leverage your author platform to promote your books by sharing excerpts, behind-the-scenes content, book trailers, or offering limited-time discounts. Engage with book clubs, writing groups, and literary events to gain exposure and connect with potential readers.

**Track and Adapt:** Continuously track the success of your author platform by tracking metrics such as website traffic, social media engagement, email open rates, or book sales. Analyze this data to identify areas of improvement and adjust your strategy.

Remember, building an author platform is an ongoing process that requires consistent effort and engagement. Using social media, blogs, websites, and other channels effectively, authors can connect with readers, establish a loyal following, and ultimately enhance their writing careers.

### Leveraging Reviews and Testimonials to Further Establish Authority & Credibility:

In the prevailing digital landscape, where knowledge is instantly accessible, consumers are progressively relying on reviews and testimonials to steer their buying choices. This trend holds true not just in the realm of products and services, but also in the world of information and knowledge.

For authors, bloggers, and experts in any field, leveraging positive reviews and testimonials is paramount in establishing authority and credibility. These positive endorsements act as social proof, assuring potential readers, viewers, or clients they are investing their time and money in something valuable.

One of the key benefits of gathering positive reviews and testimonials is the establishment of credibility. When readers, influencers, or experts within your field vouch for your work, it enhances your reputation and knowledge. It becomes an external validation you have the knowledge and skills to create high-quality content.

Positive reviews and testimonials can significantly boost your visibility and attract a wider audience. With the proliferation of social media platforms, people share and recommend things they find valuable or insightful. By harnessing the power of these recommendations, your work can reach a much larger audience, ultimately increasing your influence and expanding your reach.

Additionally, positive reviews and testimonials play a crucial role in building trust with your audience. When individuals see that others have had a positive experience with your content, they feel more confident in investing their time and energy in what you offer. Trust is the cornerstone of any successful relationship, and when your audience trusts you, they are more likely to engage with your work, follow your recommendations, or even become loyal customers.

So, how can you effectively leverage reviews and testimonials to bolster your authority and credibility?

First, actively encourage your readers, clients, or viewers to provide feedback through reviews and testimonials. Make it easy for them to share their thoughts by providing clear instructions or even setting up a designated testimonial page on your website.

Second, contact influential individuals within your field and ask for their feedback or endorsement. These experts can provide you with invaluable testimonials that carry significant weight and credibility. Don't be afraid to ask for their opinion – often, experts are more than willing to support fellow professionals.

Finally, once you have gathered a collection of positive reviews and testimonials, use them strategically. Incorporate snippets or quotes into your website, blog, or social media profiles to showcase the positive feedback. You can also create a dedicated section on your website where potential clients or readers can easily access and browse through these endorsements.

Leveraging reviews and testimonials is essential for anyone looking to establish authority and credibility. Positive feedback from readers, influencers, and experts enhances your reputation, builds trust, and increases your visibility. So, make it a priority to gather these endorsements and use them effectively to elevate your content, attract a wider audience, and solidify your position as an expert in your field.

### Speaking Engagements and Media Appearances to Enhance Authority & Reach A Wider Audience:

Speaking engagements and media appearances provide excellent opportunities for authors to share their knowledge and promote their self-published books. By leveraging their published works, authors can secure speaking engagements at conferences and events, as well as media appearances, enabling them to reach a wider audience and enhance their authority in the industry.

One significant benefit of leveraging self-published books is the increased credibility it brings to an author's profile. When an author has a published work, it establishes them as an expert in their field and gives them the credentials to approach event organizers and media outlets. Books are seen as a symbol of extensive knowledge, making it more likely for authors to be considered for speaking engagements and media appearances.

Speaking engagements at conferences or events provide authors with a unique opportunity to share their ideas and insights with a targeted audience. By referencing their self-published books during these engagements, authors can not only gain the attention and respect of the audience but also generate interest in their published works. Attending industry-related events also lets authors connect with like-minded professionals, potential readers, and media representatives, leading to further exposure and networking opportunities.

Media appearances, such as interviews on podcasts, television shows, or radio programs, let authors be featured in platforms with a massive audience reach. These appearances help authors extend their influence and attract potential readers who may not have come across their self-published books otherwise. Media outlets often seek experts who can provide valuable insights, and by leveraging their published works, authors can position themselves as credible sources of information, further enhancing their authority in the eyes of their audience.

To strengthen their authority and credibility, authors must actively gather positive reviews and testimonials from readers, influencers, and experts in their field. Reviews and testimonials serve as powerful social proof, reinforcing the quality and value of an author's self-published books. Readers are more likely to trust content endorsed by others, making positive reviews a powerful marketing tool.

Authors can encourage readers to leave reviews by offering incentives or conducting targeted review campaigns. Additionally, collaborating with influential individuals or experts in the field to create endorsements or testimonials amplifies an author's credibility. These positive testimonials can be highlighted on the author's website, in promotional materials, and during speaking engagements and media appearances. Such testimonials not only enhance the author's credibility but also persuade potential readers to give their self-published books a chance.

Leveraging self-published books provides authors with several benefits when securing speaking engagements at conferences or events and media appearances. By showcasing their published works, authors enhance their authority and credibility, letting them reach a wider audience and attract more readers. Gathering positive reviews and testimonials further establishes an author's authority, strengthening their profile and increasing the chances of success in the industry.

### Collaborating With Other Authors and Experts to Further Establish Authority & Credibility:

Collaborating with other authors and industry experts can be immensely beneficial when establishing authority and credibility in your field. By joining forces and leveraging each other's strengths and knowledge, you can create a powerful network that enhances your reputation and widens your reach to a broader audience. Here are a few ways collaborating with others can elevate your authority:

**Joint book projects:** Co-authoring a book with another expert or author instantly lends credibility to your work. Combining your expertise with someone else's can result in a more comprehensive and well-rounded book, attracting a larger readership and showing you are well-connected within your industry. Additionally, publishing a joint book lets you tap into each other's networks and expand your visibility.

**Podcasts:** Hosting or being a guest on a podcast with other authors or industry experts can help you showcase your knowledge and build authority among a captive audience. By engaging in high-quality discussions, you can offer valuable insights, share diverse perspectives, and prove yourself to be a thought leader in your field. Collaborating on podcasts also lets you tap into each other's fan base or followers, further expanding your reach.

**Webinars:** Collaborating on webinars enables you to leverage the knowledge of multiple authors or experts, providing attendees with a richer and more diverse learning experience. As a participant, you can showcase your knowledge alongside other well-respected professionals, leading to increased credibility and authority. Webinars often attract a broader audience since participants are drawn to the combined knowledge being offered.

**Networking opportunities:** Collaborating with other authors and experts opens doors to networking opportunities that can further enhance your authority. By attending events, conferences, or workshops together, you can meet other influential individuals in your industry, potentially leading to collaborations, speaking engagements, or joint ventures. Building relationships with other thought leaders in your field also shows you are respected among peers, strengthening your authority.

**Cross-promotion:** Collaborating with other authors or industry experts allows for cross-promotion of your work and knowledge. Supporting and promoting each other's books, podcasts, webinars, or events can significantly expand your audience and reach. By tapping into each other's networks and leveraging the power of shared platforms, you can amplify your message and credibility to a wider audience.

Collaborating with other authors and experts can be a game-changer in establishing authority and credibility. Through joint book projects, podcasts, webinars, and networking opportunities, you can harness the power of collaboration to enhance your reputation, widen your reach, and solidify your position as an industry expert. Embrace these opportunities for collaboration, and watch as your authority and credibility soar to new heights.

**Case Study: How a Book Helped Emma Grow Her Dog Grooming Business** (This story is a fictional example for illustrative purposes)

Emma Clark has always had a passion for dogs. She started working part-time as a dog groomer 10 years ago while attending community college. Emma turned her part-time gig into a full-time small business after graduating.

Emma ran a modest dog grooming studio, relying on word-of-mouth and social media for customers. Her annual revenue was stagnant at around $75,000 with little growth. Emma wanted to expand her client base and annual income.

In 2021, Emma wrote a book about her career as a dog groomer. She wanted to share insider tips while expressing her love for the craft. The book was titled "A Dog's Best Friend: Confessions of a Passionate Pet Groomer."

Emma faced several obstacles during the writing process. As a busy entrepreneur, it was a struggle to find time to write. Organizing her decade of experience into a book structure also proved challenging. Emma persevered and completed writing the book after 9 months.

After self-publishing the book, Emma heavily promoted it on social media and offered free copies to new email subscribers. Local pet stores agreed to sell the book. Everything seemed to be going well.

Unexpectedly, a local news article accused Emma of sharing trade secrets. Some fellow groomers criticized her book as revealing too many insider tips. The negative publicity was upsetting and stressful for Emma.

Despite this setback, Emma continued marketing her book. She donated copies to animal shelters to highlight her mission of supporting all dogs. Positive word-of-mouth from shelter employees and pet owners offset the earlier controversy.

Within a year, Emma sold over 3,000 copies of her book. Many readers became loyal customers, allowing Emma to double her annual revenue to $150,000. By sharing her passion, the book let Emma grow her business while staying true to her love of dogs.

**From Emma...**

Writing A Dog's Best Friend was a journey that challenged me in unexpected ways. As a lifelong dog lover, I was excited to share my passion for grooming through a book. I hoped it would let me grow my business while expressing my appreciation for dogs. However, I encountered hurdles along the way.

The writing process tested my time management and perseverance. Juggling it amidst running a business was grueling. Organizing so many stories and tips into coherent chapters required patience and discipline. But pushing through those struggles to finish the book taught me I'm capable of more than I thought.

The criticism from a few fellow groomers after publication was difficult. I can understand how some viewed it as revealing trade secrets. My intent was solely to help dog owners appreciate the care that goes into grooming. The accusations felt hurtful given my pure motivations. However, the experience showed me I can't please everyone. Staying true to my values was most important.

What matters most is the book lets me share my authentic passion with kindred spirits. The positive feedback from appreciative readers, shelters, and pet owners has been so heartwarming. Growing my business was important, but bonding with dog lovers made the effort worthwhile.

I've learned to focus on the joy writing A Dog's Best Friend has brought me and so many readers. Though the path had challenges, the journey deepened my commitment to dogs and this career I love. Writing from the heart requires courage to be vulnerable, but the connections formed make it all worthwhile. I'm thankful this experience expanded my skills, thickened my skin, and strengthened my voice.

**Chapter Summary:**

The chapter discusses the rise of self-publishing as an empowering tool for authors to establish themselves as experts and authorities. It highlights the evolving publishing landscape and how self-publishing provides more control, autonomy, and opportunities for personal brand building compared to traditional publishing.

Choosing the right niche to specialize in is emphasized to show knowledge. Writing high-quality, well-researched content proves knowledge and engages readers. Building an author platform through social media, blogging, email marketing, and collaborations connects authors to readers.

Leveraging reviews and testimonials from readers and experts builds credibility and trust. Securing speaking engagements and media appearances through published works expands reach and authority.

Finally, collaborating on book projects, podcasts, webinars, and networking with other authors and industry experts enhances credibility and expands visibility.

Overall, the chapter outlines strategies for using self-publishing to showcase expertise, establish authority, connect with readers, and position oneself as a thought leader.

**In our next chapter...**

In the upcoming chapter, we underscore the significance of fostering an engaged audience even before your book is ready to launch.

We guide you through the process of identifying your target audience, encapsulating the importance of comprehensive market research based on demographics, psychographics, and understanding your audience's needs and preferences.

We delve into the strategic use of social media platforms like Facebook, Twitter, Instagram, YouTube, and Goodreads to establish a dynamic presence and engage your audience.

The chapter also provides insight into creating captivating, value-driven content with compelling hooks, insightful narratives, appealing visuals, and interactive elements. You'll learn how to build your email list through enticing lead magnets, effective sign-up forms, and the power of segmentation and automation for personalized engagement.

We'll also discuss how collaborations with influencers can amplify your reach and explore the benefits of hosting live events and virtual book tours to foster meaningful connections with your readers. Key benefits such as enhanced visibility, immediate feedback, networking opportunities, accessibility, and increased engagement are explored in depth.

This chapter serves as a practical guide, brimming with strategies to build an engaged audience, crafting compelling content, effectively leveraging social platforms and email marketing, and hosting interactive events to spark excitement and loyalty leading to your book launch. Don't miss out!

~

## CHAPTER EIGHT

# BUILDING AN ENGAGED AUDIENCE AND PLATFORM FOR BOOK LAUNCH SUCCESS

Understanding **The Importance of Building an Engaged Audience:**

In this chapter, we will explore the crucial role of having a strong and engaged audience before launching a book. A book's success depends not only on its content but also on the receptiveness and enthusiasm of its readers. Therefore, understanding the significance of building an engaged audience is crucial for authors and publishers alike. By the end of this chapter, you will have a clear understanding of how an active and committed audience can be the driving force behind the success of any book.

**Defining an Engaged Audience:**

To comprehend the importance of building an engaged audience, we must first establish what it means to have an engaged audience. An engaged audience consists of individuals who actively participate in and connect with an author's work. They regularly consume the author's content, interact with the author and fellow readers, and demonstrate a genuine interest in the subject matter.

**The Key to a Book's Success:**

An engaged audience acts as the cornerstone of a book's success. They provide vital support to authors by spreading the word, generating buzz, and creating a sense of anticipation for the book's release. Without a solid base of engaged readers, the book may struggle to gain traction in the crowded literary marketplace.

**Building Trust and Credibility:**

One of the primary benefits of building an engaged audience is the development of trust and credibility with readers. By consistently delivering valuable content and engaging with their audience, authors can establish themselves as trustworthy sources of information in their niche. This trust acts as a magnet, attracting more readers who are eager to experience the author's work firsthand.

**Early Feedback and Beta Readers:**

An engaged audience also plays a crucial role in the pre-publication phase of a book. Authors can leverage their audience by seeking early feedback on drafts, utilizing beta readers, and conducting surveys. This valuable input enables authors to fine-tune their work, address potential issues, and improve the overall quality of their book.

**Word-of-Mouth Promotion:**

Engaged readers are likely to become passionate advocates for an author's work. They willingly share their enthusiasm with friends, family, and social media followers, thus becoming valuable ambassadors for the book. Word-of-mouth promotion is a powerful force, providing authors with organic exposure to new audiences and increasing the chances of wider recognition and book sales.

**Long-Term Relationship Building:**

Building an engaged audience is not a one-time endeavor; it fosters long-term relationships with readers. Through consistent communication, authors can build a sustainable community of supporters who remain engaged beyond the launch of a single book. This loyal audience becomes a powerful asset for future projects and ensures an author's continued success.

The significance of building an engaged audience cannot be overstated. Authors who prioritize developing and nurturing a strong relationship with their readers significantly increase their chances of success. An engaged audience provides authors with support, feedback, promotion, and long-term sustainability. By recognizing the importance of building an engaged audience, authors can position themselves for a successful book launch and a rewarding writing career.

### Identifying and Defining Your Target Audience:

To successfully build a platform that resonates with readers, it is crucial to have a clear understanding of your target audience. This chapter aims to provide guidance on how to effectively identify and define your target audience. By homing in on the specific characteristics and needs of your target audience, you can tailor your content and messaging to meet their expectations and establish meaningful connections.

### Conduct Market Research:

To begin, it is essential to conduct thorough market research to gather insights about your potential readers. This research can include surveys, focus groups, analyzing competitors, and utilizing online tools to gather demographic information. By understanding the demographics, habits, preferences, and pain points of your potential readers, you can paint a clearer picture of your target audience.

### Define Psychographic Factors:

Beyond demographics, psychographic factors play a vital role in understanding your target audience. These factors encompass individuals' interests, values, opinions, and behaviors. To define psychographic factors, consider conducting in-depth interviews, analyzing social media conversations, or creating user personas. This information will help you understand the motivations behind your readers' actions and align your platform's messaging accordingly.

### Identify Pain Points and Needs:

To resonate with your target audience, it is essential to identify their pain points and unmet needs. These can be discovered through market research, surveys, or by engaging directly with your readers through social media or feedback channels. Understanding what challenges your audience faces will enable you to craft content that provides relevant solutions and addresses their concerns.

**Segment Your Audience:**

In some cases, your target audience may be quite diverse, making it necessary to segment them based on key characteristics or preferences. By dividing your audience into smaller groups, you can personalize your content to better suit their specific needs. Segmenting your audience could be based on age, location, interests, or any other relevant factor identified during your research.

**Create User Personas:**

User personas are fictional representations of your ideal readers, created based on real data collected during your research. These personas encompass demographic information, psychographic traits, motivations, and pain points. Having user personas will allow you to envision and empathize with the specific individuals you aim to reach, helping you create content that resonates on a deeper level.

**Continuously Refine and Update:**

Remember that understanding your target audience is an ongoing process. As your platform evolves and new trends emerge, it is crucial to continuously refine and update your knowledge of your readers. Engage with your audience through social media, conduct regular surveys, and monitor analytical data to ensure that your platform remains relevant to their evolving needs and preferences.

By identifying and defining your target audience effectively, you can take decisive steps toward building a successful platform that resonates with your readers. Conducting thorough market research, defining psychographic factors, understanding pain points and needs, segmenting your audience, creating user personas, and continuously refining your understanding of your readers are all crucial steps in this process. Investing time and effort into gaining a deep understanding of your target audience will yield invaluable results, enabling you to connect with your readers on a meaningful level and cultivate a loyal following.

**Utilizing Social Media Platforms to Engage with Readers:**

In today's digital age, social media platforms have revolutionized how authors connect and engage with their audience. The accessibility and reach of these platforms allow authors to create a powerful online presence and establish genuine connections with their readers. This chapter aims to guide authors in effectively utilizing various social media platforms to connect, engage, and grow their audience.

**Understanding the Different Social Media Platforms:**

**a. Facebook:** With over 2.8 billion monthly active users, Facebook offers a wide range of features to connect with readers. Create an author page to showcase your work, interact through comments and direct messages, and join relevant writing groups to network with fellow authors and potential readers.

**b. X 'the social media platform formerly known as Twitter':** Known for its succinct messaging, Twitter allows authors to share updates, hold live Q&A sessions, and participate in writing-related conversations using relevant hashtags. Utilize Twitter as a platform for quick communication and engage with readers through retweets, replies, and direct messages.

**c. Instagram:** A visually focused platform, Instagram enables authors to share behind-the-scenes glimpses of their writing routine, book covers, events, and quotes to captivate their audience. Utilize relevant hashtags, create visually appealing content, and engage with followers through likes, comments, and direct messages.

**d. YouTube:** Video content is gaining immense popularity, making YouTube an essential platform for authors. Create a channel to share writing advice, book trailers, author interviews, or reading excerpts. Engage with viewers through comments and collaborate with other authors or influencers to expand your reach.

**e. Goodreads:** As a social media platform specifically designed for readers and authors, Goodreads allows authors to connect with their target audience more effectively. Create an author profile, interact with readers through comments and reviews, join niche book clubs, and host virtual book events. Goodreads is owned and operated by Amazon.

**2. Establishing an Active Online Presence:**

**a. Consistency & Quality:** Regularly post valuable and engaging content, such as writing tips, book recommendations, and updates about upcoming projects. Make sure your content is authentic, well-written, and aligns with your brand.

**b. Visual Appeal:** Utilize appealing visuals, such as high-quality book cover images, aesthetically pleasing photos, and graphics to stand out in a crowded digital environment. Ensure your visual content reflects your writing style and brand identity.

c. Interact and Respond: Actively engage with your audience by responding to comments, addressing queries, and participating in discussions related to your writing niche. Show genuine interest in your readers, fostering a sense of community and loyalty.

**d. Cross-Promote:** Leverage the power of cross-promotion by sharing your social media handles across platforms. Encourage readers to connect with you on multiple platforms to maximize your reach and engagement.

**3. Engaging Strategies for Each Platform:**

**a. Contests and Giveaways:** Conduct writing contests or book give-aways on platforms like Facebook, Twitter, or Instagram to generate excitement and reward your audience for their support. This fosters engagement, attracts new readers, and helps spread the word about your work.

**b. Live Events:** Host live Q&A sessions or book discussions through platforms like Facebook Live, YouTube Live, or Instagram Live. This interactive approach allows you to answer readers' questions, provide insights into your writing process, and strengthen the bond with your audience.

**c. Storytelling:** Utilize platforms like Instagram and Facebook Stories to share authentic, behind-the-scenes content. Show snippets of your writing process, book launch preparations, or events you attend. This personal touch creates a connection and builds anticipation among your audience.

**d. Collaborations:** Partner with other authors, influencers, or book-related businesses to expand your reach and tap into new audiences. Collaborative projects, such as guest blog posts, joint giveaways, or co-hosted events, offer fresh perspectives and increased exposure.

Social media platforms offer authors an invaluable opportunity to connect, engage, and cultivate a dedicated audience. By understanding different platforms, establishing an active online presence, and implementing engaging strategies, authors can effectively utilize social media to build meaningful relationships with their readers. Embrace these platforms as powerful tools, and let your voice be heard, creating lasting connections in the digital writing community.

### Creating Compelling Content That Keeps Readers Coming Back for More:

In today's digital era, where content is abundant, authors and creators face the challenge of grabbing and holding onto their audience's attention. To stand out from the crowd, it is essential to consistently produce compelling and valuable content that entices readers to keep coming back for more. In this chapter, we will explore various tips and techniques to help you create engaging content that captivates your audience.

### Know Your Audience:

One of the most critical aspects of creating compelling content is understanding your target audience. Take the time to research and gather insights about their preferences, interests, and pain points. By developing a deep understanding of your readers, you can tailor your content specifically to resonate with them.

### Begin with a Strong Hook:

To grab your audience's attention from the start, it is crucial to have a powerful and captivating opening. Start with an intriguing question, a thought-provoking statement, or a fascinating anecdote that immediately piques their curiosity. A strong hook will entice readers to continue exploring your content.

### Deliver Unique and Valuable Insights:

To make your content compelling, go beyond the surface level and provide unique perspectives and insights. Conduct thorough research, interview experts, or share personal experiences that offer something new and valuable to your audience. This added depth and value will keep readers engaged and make them feel like they are gaining something from consuming your content.

### Utilize Storytelling Techniques:

People love stories. Weaving storytelling techniques into your content creates an emotional connection with your audience. Use vivid and descriptive language, evoke empathy through relatable characters or personal experiences, and build suspense to keep readers invested. The power of storytelling will resonate deeply with your audience and keep them eagerly turning the pages.

### Use Visuals to Enhance Engagement:

Visuals play a crucial role in capturing and retaining your audience's attention. Incorporate relevant images, infographics, or videos to break up the text and make your content more visually appealing. Ensure the visuals align with your message and enhance the overall understanding and engagement of your audience.

### Encourage Interaction and Conversation:

Engaging content should initiate a dialogue with your readers. Encourage them to leave comments, ask questions, or share their opinions. Respond to their feedback and create a space where conversations can flourish. By fostering a sense of community, you create a more interactive and engaging content experience.

**Optimize for Readability:**

Long paragraphs and dense blocks of text can quickly discourage readers. Optimize your content for readability by using subheadings, bullet points, and concise sentences. Break up complex ideas into manageable chunks, making it easier for readers to consume and retain information. Additionally, consider using formatting options that enhance readability, such as bolding key points or using different font sizes or colors.

Creating compelling and engaging content requires careful consideration of your audience's needs and desires. By incorporating the tips and techniques mentioned in this chapter, you can consistently produce valuable content that captivates readers and keeps them coming back for more. Remember, the key to success lies in understanding your audience, delivering unique insights, utilizing storytelling, incorporating visuals, fostering conversation, and optimizing for readability. With these strategies in your arsenal, you can create an irresistible content experience that leaves a lasting impact.

**Building An Email List: Nurturing and Engaging with Your Audience:**

Email marketing continues to be one of the most influential and effective ways to connect with your target audience. By building and maintaining a dedicated email list, authors can nurture relationships, engage readers, and promote their work in a more personalized and direct manner.

In this section, we will provide you with a comprehensive guide on how to successfully build and maintain an email list, along with strategies for effective email marketing.

**Understand your target audience:** Before starting an email list, it's essential to define your target audience. Understand their needs, preferences, and interests to create valuable content that they will find appealing.

**Choose a reliable email service provider (ESP):** An ESP will help you manage your email campaigns, automate processes, and track the performance of your emails. Popular options include Mailchimp, ConvertKit, and Constant Contact.

**Create compelling lead magnets:** To entice visitors to join your email list, offer them valuable content in exchange for their email address. This can include free e-books, exclusive content, or access to a private community. Make sure your lead magnets align with your audience's interests.

**Optimize your website for email sign-ups:** Place prominent sign-up forms, or "opt-in" forms, on your website to capture visitor emails. Use eye-catching design elements and compelling call to action phrases to encourage sign-ups.

**Promote your email list on social media:** Leverage your social media platforms to promote your email list effectively. Create engaging posts and share sneak peeks of exclusive content to attract potential subscribers.

**Use pop-ups and timed slide-ins:** Consider utilizing exit-intent pop-ups or slide-ins to capture the attention of visitors who are about to leave your website. Offer them a last-minute opportunity to join your email list.

**Implement double opt-in:** A double opt-in process requires users to confirm their subscription by clicking a link in a confirmation email. This ensures that your email list consists of engaged and interested subscribers.

**Segment your email list:** Categorize your subscribers based on their interests, preferences, or any other relevant criteria. Segmenting allows you to deliver more personalized content, increasing engagement and conversion rates.

**Plan an email content strategy:** Develop a consistent email content strategy that provides value to your subscribers. This can include sharing updates, exclusive content, behind-the-scenes insights, or exclusive discounts.

**Automate email campaigns:** Set up automated email sequences, such as welcome emails, nurture series, or abandoned cart reminders. Automation saves time, ensures timely communication, and increases the chances of conversions.

**Analyze and optimize performance:** Regularly track and analyze the performance of your email campaigns. Pay attention to open rates, click-through rates, and conversion rates. Experiment with different subject lines, email templates, and call-to-actions to optimize your results.

**Maintain a healthy email list:** Regularly clean your email list by removing inactive or disengaged subscribers. This ensures that your list remains targeted, engaged, and receptive to your messages.

By implementing these strategies, authors can build a robust email list that serves as a direct line of communication with their audience. Mastering email marketing will allow you to nurture relationships, engage readers, and promote your work effectively.

**Collaborating With Influencers and To Expand Reach & Engage with New Readers:**

The advent of social media has given rise to influential individuals and bloggers who have successfully built engaged audiences. Leveraging the reach and credibility of these influencers can prove to be a game-changer for book launches. In this chapter, we will delve into the various methods and strategies for effectively collaborating with influencers and bloggers, ultimately expanding your reach and engaging with new readers.

**Identify Relevant Influencers and Bloggers:**

The first step is to identify influencers and bloggers who resonate with your book's genre or niche. Research popular bloggers, Instagram-mers, YouTubers, or podcast hosts who have a substantial following and an engaged audience that aligns with your target readers. Look for influencers who frequently share content related to books, reading, or your book's genre, as they are more likely to resonate with your message.

### Build Genuine Relationships:

Once you have identified potential influencers and bloggers, focus on building genuine relationships with them. Engage with their content by liking, sharing, and commenting on their posts. Show a sincere interest in their work to establish rapport. It is important to approach collaborations with influencers and bloggers as partnerships rather than one-time transactions. Building a long-term relationship will yield better results for your book launch.

### Provide Advance Copies and Exclusive Content:

Offer influencers and bloggers advance copies of your book to read and review before its official release. This grants them exclusive access to your content, making them feel valued and incentivizing them to promote your book. Additionally, share exclusive content related to your book, such as behind-the-scenes glimpses or author interviews, which they can share with their audience.

### Guest Blogging and Influencer Takeovers:

Invite influencers and bloggers to guest blog on your website or take over your social media accounts for a day. This allows them to showcase their expertise or share their experiences with your audience. This mutually beneficial arrangement expands both your reach and theirs while authentically engaging with new readers.

### Sponsored Posts and Affiliate Programs:

Consider sponsoring influencer posts or offering affiliate programs to incentivize influencers and bloggers to promote your book. Sponsored posts involve paying influencers to create content featuring your book, while affiliate programs offer influencers a percentage of sales generated through their unique affiliate links. Ensure that these promotional posts are disclosed as sponsored to maintain transparency and trust with their audience.

## Collaborative Events and Giveaways:

Collaborate with influencers and bloggers to host virtual or in-person events related to your book. These could include live Q&A sessions, panel discussions, or virtual book tours with influencer interviews. Additionally, organize collaborative giveaways where influencers and bloggers offer their audience the chance to win copies of your book, further increasing its visibility and generating excitement.

## Leverage User-Generated Content:

Encourage influencers and bloggers to create user-generated content based on your book. This could be in the form of book reviews, unboxing videos, or recommendations on their platforms. Share this content with your audience and leverage it to generate social proof and trust among potential readers.

Collaborating with influencers and bloggers provides an invaluable opportunity to expand your reach and engage with new readers during your book launch. By identifying relevant influencers, building genuine relationships, and offering exclusive content, you can leverage their existing engaged audience to create buzz around your book. Additionally, through sponsored posts, affiliate programs, collaborative events, and leveraging user-generated content, you can further amplify your book's visibility and increase its chances of success. Embrace the power of influencers and bloggers to tap into the online book community and propel your book launch to new heights.

## Harnessing The Power of Live Events and Virtual Book Tours:

Connecting with readers is an essential part of an author's journey. While writing a compelling book is crucial, creating a personal connection with your audience is equally important. Live events and virtual book tours provide the perfect platform to engage with readers in a meaningful way, fostering relationships, and building a devoted fan base. In this chapter, we will explore the benefits of hosting live events and virtual book tours and provide practical advice on how to organize successful and engaging events.

**Benefits of Hosting Live Events:**

**Personal Connection:** Live events allow authors to interact with readers face-to-face, fostering a personal connection that goes beyond the written words. This connection creates a lasting impression and strengthens the bond between author and reader.

Increased Visibility: Live events provide an opportunity for authors to increase their visibility and reach a broader audience. Public speaking engagements, book signings, and panel discussions can attract media attention, leading to enhanced publicity and the potential for new readers to discover your book.

**Immediate Feedback:** Live events allow authors to receive immediate feedback from their audience. This feedback can be valuable for understanding reader perspectives, gauging reactions to your work, and gaining insights for future projects.

**Networking Opportunities:** Live events offer a chance to network with fellow authors, industry professionals, and potential collaborators. These connections can lead to future opportunities, such as joint book promotions or partnerships, expanding your reach even further.

**Practical Advice for Organizing Successful Live Events:**

**Define Your Objective:** Determine the purpose of your live event – whether it's promoting a newly released book, engaging with existing readers, or reaching a new audience. Clarifying your objective will guide your event planning and ensure it aligns with your goals.

**Select an Appropriate Venue:** Choose a venue that complements your event's objective and target audience. Consider factors such as capacity, atmosphere, and accessibility. Whether it's a bookstore, library, conference center, or a community space – select a venue that suits your needs.

**Plan Engaging Activities:** Make your event memorable by incorporating interactive and engaging activities. Consider including author readings, panel discussions, Q&A sessions, book signings, or even workshops related to your book's theme.

**Promote and Market:** Utilize both traditional and digital marketing channels to promote your live event. Leverage social media platforms, your author website, and email newsletters to spread the word. Collaborating with influencers or local media can also help increase event visibility.

**Practice and Prepare:** Rehearse your speaking engagement, readings, and any other activities beforehand to ensure smooth execution. Organize the necessary materials, such as promotional materials and books for signing, well in advance.

### Virtual Book Tours: Expanding Your Reach Online:

In addition to live events, virtual book tours are gaining popularity as a cost-effective way to connect with a broader audience. Virtual book tours involve hosting online events such as webinars, author interviews, podcasts, or social media takeovers. The benefits of virtual book tours include:

**Accessibility:** Virtual book tours eliminate geographical barriers, enabling authors to engage with readers worldwide without the need for travel. This accessibility expands your potential audience exponentially.

**Convenience:** Virtual book tours provide flexibility and convenience for both authors and attendees. Participants can join from the comfort of their homes, making it easier for readers with busy schedules to be part of the event.

**Increased Engagement:** Online events often provide opportunities for increased attendee engagement, as participants can ask questions, leave comments, and interact with the author and other attendees through chat functions or live discussions.

### Practical Advice for Organizing Successful Virtual Book Tours:

**Choose the Right Platforms:** Select the online platforms that align with your target audience and event format. Options include social media platforms (Facebook Live, Instagram Live, Twitter chats), live video streaming platforms (YouTube Live, Twitch), or dedicated webinar tools (Zoom, GoToWebinar).

**Create an Engaging Schedule:** Plan a well-structured schedule for your virtual book tour, ensuring a variety of activities that capture attendees' interest. This may include live readings, author interviews, interactive Q&A sessions, or giveaways to create excitement.

**Utilize Collaborations:** Collaborate with influencers, book bloggers, or fellow authors to co-host or promote your virtual book tour. Their followers can help expand your reach, and their expertise can enhance the event experience for attendees.

**Leverage Media:** Pitch your virtual book tour to relevant media outlets, bloggers, or podcasters. Offer interviews or guest articles to generate buzz and attract a wider audience.

**Chapter Summary:**

The chapter emphasizes the importance of building an engaged audience before launching a book, as they provide support through promotion, feedback, and loyalty.

Steps are provided for identifying your target audience through market research of demographics, psychographics, needs, and preferences.

Using social media platforms like Facebook, Twitter, Instagram, YouTube, and Goodreads to establish an active presence and implement engaging strategies is advised.

Creating valuable, story-driven content with strong hooks, insights, visuals, and interaction is recommended to captivate readers. Building an email list through lead magnets, sign-up forms, segmentation, and automation enables personalized engagement.

Collaborating with influencers through relationships, exclusive content, and events expands reach. Harnessing live events and virtual book tours fosters meaningful connections with readers.

Key benefits highlighted include visibility, immediate feedback, networking, accessibility, and increased engagement.

Overall, the chapter provides practical guidance on building an engaged audience, crafting compelling content, leveraging social platforms and email, and hosting interactive events to drive excitement and loyalty leading to launch.

**In our next chapter…**

In the upcoming chapter, we impart the significance of creating a compelling personal brand as a self-published author.

We underline the power of a unique voice and style, and the effective use of social media platforms like Facebook, Instagram, Twitter, YouTube, LinkedIn, and Goodreads to foster connections with your target audience, establish relationships, and promote your work.

The chapter offers tactical advice on engaging book bloggers and reviewers through intriguing pitches, strategy for relationship building, and understanding of their time constraints.

The importance of an eye-catching book cover, resonating with your genre and target audience, is emphasized for attracting readers. We guide you through crafting an appealing book description comprising attention-grabbing hooks, unique selling points, emotional appeal, succinct text, and a call to action.

The benefits of hosting virtual book launches and author events are discussed, highlighting their extended reach, flexibility, and accessibility. The critical role of email marketing is underscored, with insights on building a list through appealing lead magnets and optimized opt-in forms for targeted campaigns and higher engagement.

SHARE WHAT YOU KNOW:

This chapter provides you with a comprehensive overview of promotional strategies across social media, blogger outreach, virtual events, email marketing, and visual elements, all aimed at increasing awareness about your self-published book and fostering connections with readers.

~

## CHAPTER NINE

# EFFECTIVE MARKETING AND PROMOTION STRATEGIES FOR SELF-PUBLISHED BOOKS

**BUILDING A Personal Brand as A Self-Published Author: Showcasing Your Unique Voice & Style to Attract Readers:**

In the world of self-publishing, creating a strong personal brand is an essential element for success. As an author, your personal brand is the unique voice and style that sets you apart from others. It is what attracts readers, establishes credibility, and enables you to build a loyal following. In this section, we will explore the importance of developing a personal brand and discuss effective strategies to showcase your unique voice and style.

**Why Is Personal Branding Important for Self-published Authors?**

**Differentiation:** With self-publishing becoming increasingly popular, the market is saturated with authors vying for attention. A strong personal brand lets you stand out from the crowd and make a lasting impression on potential readers.

**Credibility and Trust:** Personal branding establishes trust and credibility among readers. When you consistently deliver high-quality content, engage with your audience, and maintain a distinct voice and style, readers will perceive you as a reliable and authentic author.

**Engaged Fan Base:** Building a personal brand lets you cultivate a loyal fan base. Readers who resonate with your unique voice and style will become your strongest advocates, eagerly sharing your work with others and eagerly awaiting your future publications.

Now, let's dive into some effective strategies to effectively showcase your unique voice and style to attract readers.

**Define Your Brand Identity:** Start by identifying your values, beliefs, and the features that make your writing unique. Is it your wit, sense of humor, or emotional depth? Pinpoint what sets you apart and how you want your audience to perceive you.

**Connect with Your Target Audience:** Understand who your target audience is and what they are looking for in their reading material. Tailor your content, tone, and messaging to resonate with the needs and interests of your readers. Engage with them through social media, email newsletters, or author websites to build meaningful connections.

**Consistency in Messaging:** Consistency is key when it comes to personal branding. Make sure your writing, social media presence, website design, and overall aesthetic align with your brand identity. This will reinforce your unique voice and style, making it easier for readers to identify and remember you.

**Quality Content Creation:** Focus on consistently delivering high-quality content that reflects your personal brand. Whether it's blog posts, guest articles, or social media updates, make sure your writing is consistent, engaging, and adds value to your readers' lives. This will further establish you as an expert in your niche and build trust with your audience.

**Engage and Interact:** Build a genuine connection with your readers by engaging and interacting with them. Respond to comments, messages, and emails promptly. Share insights, behind-the-scenes stories, or personal anecdotes to make readers feel more connected to you and your brand.

**Leverage Social Media:** Utilize various social media platforms to showcase your unique voice and style. Share snippets of your writing, host live reading sessions, participate in conversations, or collaborate with other authors to expand your reach. Social media lets you establish a personal connection with readers and show your brand's essence.

Building a strong personal brand as a self-published author is a long-term investment. It requires consistency, engagement, and a deep understanding of your target audience. By showcasing your unique voice and style, you have the power to attract readers, establish credibility, and build a loyal following. So, embrace your individuality, and let your personal brand shine through your writing to leave an ever-lasting impression on your readers.

**Using Social Media to Connect With Your Target Audience, Build Relationships, And Promote Your Book:**

Social media has become an integral part of our daily lives, offering a multitude of platforms for individuals and businesses to connect and share information. As an author, leveraging social media effectively can help you reach your target audience, build meaningful relationships, and promote your book successfully. Let's explore some popular platforms and strategies to harness their power.

**Facebook:** With over 2.8 billion monthly active users, Facebook presents an enormous opportunity to connect with readers. Create an engaging and professional Facebook page for your book, sharing updates, excerpts, and links to buy. Join relevant groups where your target audience congregates, actively participate, and offer valuable insights while subtly promoting your book.

**Instagram:** Known for its visually appealing nature, Instagram is an ideal platform to showcase your book cover, behind-the-scenes glimpses, and author events. Use relevant hashtags to increase visibility and engage with your followers by replying to comments and direct messages. Collaborate with influential bookstagrammers, conduct giveaways, and organize live Q&A sessions to connect even further.

**X aka Twitter:** As a platform for quick, concise messages, Twitter provides an excellent way to engage with your audience. Share updates, quotes from your book, links to articles, and retweet positive reviews. Use hashtags relevant to your book's genre, participate in writing-related Twitter chats, and follow influential figures in the literary world to stay connected.

**YouTube:** If you enjoy creating video content, consider starting a YouTube channel to provide deeper insights into your book's themes, characters, or your writing process. Share book trailers, interviews, and readings to captivate your audience. Collaborate with other authors or booktubers for cross-promotion and wider reach.

**LinkedIn:** While primarily a platform for professional networking, LinkedIn presents opportunities for authors to establish credibility and contact industry professionals. Create an informative profile that showcases your writing experience, guest blog posts, and publishing accomplishments. Engage in industry-related discussions, join writing groups, and network with fellow authors, agents, and publishers.

**Goodreads:** A platform exclusively for book lovers, Goodreads lets you connect directly with readers, showcase your work, and receive feedback. Create an author profile, establish a bookshelf, and participate in book clubs or Q&A sessions. Encourage readers to leave reviews and ratings, and interact with them by responding to comments.

**To Effectively Leverage Social Media Across Platforms:**

**Create consistent brand messaging:** Develop a unique author persona and maintain consistent branding across your social media profiles.

**Engage and reciprocate:** Interact genuinely with your audience by replying to comments, asking questions, and participating in discussions. Reciprocate engagement by supporting fellow authors and amplifying their work.

**Provide valuable content:** Offer a mix of promotional and non-promotional content, including author insights, industry news, writing tips, and book recommendations.

**Schedule and automate:** Utilize social media management tools to schedule posts in advance, ensuring a steady flow of content without overwhelming yourself.

Social media is not a one-way communication channel; it's a place to build relationships. Invest time in understanding your target audience, adapting your strategies and using social media as a platform for authentic conversations that foster connections and promote your book effectively.

## Engaging With Book Bloggers and Reviewers: Building Positive Relationships & Spreading the Word About Your Self-Published Book

In the digital era, book bloggers and reviewers wield significant influence in the literary world, with the power to expand the audience and impact of self-published titles. However, successfully approaching and engaging with these key individuals can be a daunting task. To help navigate this process with confidence, we've gathered insights on how to effectively connect with book bloggers and reviewers, including tips on writing compelling pitches and building positive relationships.

### Research and Target the Right Bloggers and Reviewers:

Before reaching out to book bloggers and reviewers, take the time to research and identify those whose interests align with your book's genre, themes, or target audience. Seek bloggers who have reviewed books like yours and have a substantial following. Personalize your selection process to increase the likelihood of a mutually beneficial collaboration.

### Create a Compelling Pitch:

A well-crafted pitch can significantly increase your chances of capturing a blogger or reviewer's attention. Consider these tips to make your pitch stand out:

**a. Personalize:** Address the blogger or reviewer by their name, showing you have taken the time to research their work and interests. Generic mass emails are less likely to generate a positive response.

**b. Highlight Relevance:** Clearly articulate why your book relates to the blogger's audience. Choose a particular part of your book that aligns with the blogger's interests or earlier content, displaying your understanding of their platform.

**c. Be Concise:** Keep your pitch succinct and engaging. Avoid over-whelming the recipient with unnecessary details – the goal is to generate curiosity and interest.

**d. Offer Benefits:** Mention any additional content or materials you could provide to help the blogger or reviewer create engaging content, such as author interviews, exclusive excerpts, or giveaways. Make it clear that you're invested in their success as well.


**Establish Genuine Relationships:**

Building authentic relationships is essential to a successful engagement with book bloggers and reviewers. Follow these steps to nurture positive connections:

**a. Read and Engage with Their Content:** Familiarize yourself with the blogger or reviewer's work by reading and commenting on their posts. Genuine interactions show your interest and commitment to their platform.

**b. Be Respectful of Their Time:** Understand that bloggers and reviewers receive many requests and have limited time. Send your pitch in a polite and concise manner and avoid follow-up emails.

**c. Show Gratitude:** Once a blogger or reviewer has agreed to feature your book or write a review, express your gratitude. A personalized thank-you email, or a social media shout-out highlights your appreciation and strengthens the connection.

**d. Share Their Content:** Support the bloggers and reviewers by promoting their content on your social media platforms or website. Collaboration and reciprocation reinforce positive relationships and encourage future collaborations.

**Follow Submission Guidelines:**

Each blogger or reviewer may have specific submission guidelines or preferences. Pay attention to their instructions regarding the format, content, and timeline for book submissions. Failing to follow their guidelines could result in rejection or the perception of disinterest in their platform.

**Be Open to Constructive Feedback:**

Reviews, whether positive or critical, offer valuable insight into readers' opinions. Be open to receiving constructive feedback from book bloggers and reviewers. Use their suggestions to improve your future writing and publishing endeavors. A willingness to learn and grow shows professionalism, and it may encourage bloggers to continue supporting your work.

Engaging with book bloggers and reviewers is a crucial step to spreading the word about your self-published book. By personalizing your pitches, building positive relationships, and valuing their feedback, you can establish a supportive network that will help increase your book's visibility and reach a wider audience. Remember, these individuals are passionate about literature, so treating them with respect and kindness will go a long way in fostering fruitful collaborations.

**Creating Eye-Catching Book Covers: Capturing Readers' Attention for Success:**

As the saying goes, "Don't judge a book by its cover." However, in the world of publishing, this advice often falls on deaf ears. The reality is that a book cover is one of the most critical elements in attracting readers, generating interest, and ultimately boosting sales. It serves as a visual gateway, enticing potential readers to pick up your book and take a closer look. To ensure your book gets the attention it deserves, let's explore the significance of an appealing book cover and provide guidance on how to design or hire a professional to create a visually striking cover.

Foremost, an eye-catching book cover is paramount because it communicates your book's content, genre, and tone at a glance. A well-designed cover captures the essence of your story, leaving potential readers intrigued and eager to delve into the pages within. A professionally crafted cover establishes credibility for your work, assuring readers that the book's content matches its quality. A cover that reflects the effort and care put into your writing sets the stage for a positive reading experience. A visually appealing cover can make or break a book's success.

If you're considering designing your own book cover, ensure you have a firm grasp of the principles of design and a clear understanding of your target audience. Begin by researching popular book covers in your genre and identify common elements or styles. This will help you brainstorm ideas while simultaneously avoiding clichés or design ideas that may not resonate with readers. Remember that simplicity often garners more attention than cluttered or overly complex designs. Choose a strong focal point, balanced composition, and a color palette that complements your book's genre and plot.

For those who lack design skills or prefer to focus only on writing, hiring a professional cover designer is a wise investment. Collaborating with a skilled designer makes sure your cover meets industry standards, resonates with your target audience, and has the power to stand out on crowded bookshelves or online platforms. When searching for a designer, review their portfolio and seek recommendations from fellow authors or reputable design agencies. Communication is key in this process, so effectively convey your vision, genre, and any specific elements you'd like to incorporate. A well-versed designer will not only bring your ideas to life but also provide valuable insights and suggestions to enhance the cover's impact.

A visually appealing book cover is a crucial element for attracting readers and capturing their attention. It conveys the essence of your story, establishes credibility, and entices potential readers to explore your book further. Whether you design your own cover or hire a professional, making sure it aligns with your genre, target audience, and industry standards is essential. By investing time, effort, and potentially some resources into creating an eye-catching cover, you increase the chances of your book standing out in a competitive market and enticing readers to take a chance on your literary masterpiece.

## Crafting An Effective Book Description: Tips for Writing Intriguing and Engaging Book Descriptions

As a self-published author, creating an enticing book description is crucial to capturing the attention of potential readers. A well-crafted description not only entices readers but also effectively conveys the essence of your book. Here are tips to help you write an effective book description that will captivate your target audience and increase your chances of engaging readers.

**Start with a catchy hook:** Begin your book description with an attention-grabbing statement or question that piques the reader's curiosity. This will compel them to continue reading and learn more about your book.

**Highlight the unique selling points:** Identify the features and elements that make your book stand out from the rest. Is it a thrilling mystery, a heartwarming romance, or a unique blend of genres? Communicate what sets your book apart and makes it compelling.

**Showcase the emotional journey:** Connect with your readers on an emotional level by conveying the emotions and experiences your characters go through. Use descriptive language to paint a vivid picture of the setting, conflicts, and relationships, creating a sense of empathy and intrigue.

**Keep it concise but engaging:** Readers often skim through book descriptions, so it's essential to keep your description concise while still maintaining its appeal. Use short paragraphs, bullet points, or subheadings to break up the text and make it easy to read.

**Avoid spoilers:** While you want to tease readers with enough information to generate interest, be cautious not to reveal any major plot twists or give away the ending. Keep the focus on the central conflict and key elements without spoiling the surprises your book holds.

**Include endorsements or accolades:** If you have received positive reviews or endorsements from trusted sources, proudly display them in your book description. Such endorsements can build credibility and encourage readers to give your book a chance.

**Use powerful language and active verbs:** Craft your book description with engaging and thought-provoking language. Be concise and use active verbs to create an energetic and exciting tone that reflects the essence of your book.

**Add a call to action:** Encourage readers to take the next step by adding a clear call to action at the end of your book description. Whether it's inviting them to click the "buy now" button or suggesting they download a sample chapter, guide readers toward acting.

**Get feedback and revise:** Once you've written your book description, seek feedback from trusted friends, fellow authors, or beta readers. They can provide valuable insights and suggestions to improve the clarity and effectiveness of your description.

**Test and iterate:** As you self-publish, be open to tweaking and refining your book description based on reader feedback and market response. Pay attention to conversion rates and adjust your description ensuring your book resonates with your target audience.

A well-crafted book description can create excitement, generate interest, and drive book sales. By using these tips to create an intriguing and engaging book description, you can effectively communicate the essence of your self-published book and entice potential readers to discover the captivating world you have created.

**Organizing Virtual Book Launches and Author Events to Ensure Maximum Participation & Exposure:**

Organizing virtual book launches and online author events have become increasingly popular due to the convenience, flexibility, and global reach they offer. This section will explore the many benefits of virtual book launches and online author events and provide practical advice on organizing and promoting these events to maximize participation and exposure.

**Benefits of Virtual Book Launches and Online Author Events:**

**Global Reach:** Unlike physical events, virtual book launches and online author events have no geographical limitations. They let authors connect with readers from around the world, increasing their reach and potential readership.

**Convenience and Flexibility:** Virtual events can be attended from the comfort of one's home or office, eliminating the need for travel, accommodation, or specific time commitments. Attendees can participate at their convenience, leading to higher attendance rates.

**Cost-Effectiveness:** Organizing virtual events often incurs lower costs compared to physical events. There are no venue rentals, catering expenses, or printing costs for promotional materials, thus making it a more budget-friendly option for authors.

**Increased Accessibility for Readers:** Virtual events enhances accessibility for readers who may have physical disabilities or live in remote locations, letting them engage with authors and their works effortlessly.

**Efficient Author-Reader Interaction:** Online platforms offer various features, such as live chats, Q&A sessions, and virtual book signings, that help with direct engagement between authors and readers. This engagement promotes a sense of community and strengthens author-reader relationships.

**Organizing and Promoting Virtual Book Launches and Author Events:**

**Choose the right platform:** Select an online platform that suits the event's format and goals. Popular options include Zoom, Webex, or Facebook Live. Ensure the platform chosen can accommodate the expected number of attendees and provide necessary features like audiovisual capabilities and interactive chat functions.

**Set a date and time:** Consider different time zones to accommodate participants from various regions. Avoid scheduling conflicts with other major events and holidays. Promote the event well in advance to ensure attendees mark their calendars.

**Develop a detailed plan:** Outline the event's flow, including introductions, author presentations, Q&A sessions, and interactions with attendees. Allocate time to each segment, ensuring a balance between engagement and efficiency.

**Collaborate with influencers and book clubs:** Partnering with influencers, book clubs, or relevant websites can help promote the event. Contact social media influencers, bloggers, or podcasts that align with your book's genre or target audience. They can provide exposure and broaden your reach.

**Leverage social media and email marketing:** Create promotional materials (images, videos, or teasers) to generate excitement and share them on social media platforms. Use email newsletters to contact your existing readership and fan base, encouraging them to attend and spread the word.

**Encourage pre-registration:** Creating a landing page or event registration form can help gather attendee information and provide reminders leading to the event. Offer incentives like exclusive content or early access for pre-registered participants to boost registrations.

**Engage with attendees during the event:** Actively encourage participation and engagement throughout the event. Use live chat features to answer questions, interact with attendees, and create a sense of community. Consider incorporating interactive elements such as polls or giveaways to maintain high engagement levels.

· · ·

Virtual book launches and online author events provide authors with an array of benefits, including global reach, convenience, cost-effectiveness, increased accessibility, and efficient reader interaction. By carefully organizing and effectively promoting virtual events, authors can ensure maximum participation and exposure, connecting with readers from all corners of the world and fostering a vibrant literary community.

### Building An Email List and Running Targeted Campaigns: Unlocking the Potential of Email Marketing

In today's digital age, where social media reigns supreme, it's easy to overlook the power of email marketing. However, building and nurturing an email list remains one of the most effective strategies for engaging with your audience. Why? Because it provides a direct, personalized channel of communication that lets you connect with your readers on a more intimate level. Targeted email marketing campaigns offer a higher return on investment compared to other marketing channels. Let's explore the importance of building an email list and discover techniques to maximize its potential.

### Creating Reader Magnets: Attracting Subscribers:

The foundation of any successful email marketing campaign is a strong and growing subscriber base. To entice potential subscribers, you need to create reader magnets. These are valuable resources such as e-books, whitepapers, or exclusive content you offer in exchange for email addresses. By providing something of value, you make it enticing for readers to join your email list.

When creating reader magnets, consider your audience's pain points and interests. Craft content that addresses their needs and offers practical solutions. Research popular topics within your industry and explore ways to provide unique insights or perspectives. By continuously delivering value, you build trust and prove yourself to be an authority in your niche, leading to increased engagement and loyalty.

### Setting Up Opt-in Forms: Capturing Subscribers:

Once you have compelling reader magnets, the next step is to create opt-in forms that capture your audience's email addresses. Opt-in forms are strategically placed on your website or landing pages, prompting visitors to input their contact information. When designing these forms, simplicity is key. Keep them clutter-free, concise, and visually appealing. Focus on the benefits of subscribing rather than overwhelming visitors with excessive fields or information.

Consider using various types of opt-in forms to maximize your reach. Pop-ups, slide-ins, inline forms, or welcome mats are all effective ways to capture visitors' attention and encourage them to subscribe. By optimizing opt-in forms for mobile devices, you make sure mobile users have a seamless experience, ultimately increasing the chances of conversion.

**Targeted Email Marketing Campaigns: Reaching and Engaging:**

Now that your email list is growing, it's time to unleash the power of targeted email marketing campaigns. Segmenting your email list based on subscribers' behavior and interests lets you craft personalized campaigns that resonate with different subsets of your audience. By identifying specific groups, you can tailor content, offers, and calls to action to meet their unique needs, leading to higher engagement and conversion rates.

Automation tools are vital in running successful targeted campaigns. Use autoresponders to automate your email sequences and nurture new subscribers. Send personalized emails based on subscribers' interactions with your website or earlier emails, creating a personalized experience that drives results. By analyzing metrics such as open rates, click-through rates, and conversions, you can continuously optimize your campaigns for even greater success.

Building an email list and running targeted campaigns are essential for effective audience engagement. By offering valuable reader magnets and setting up optimized opt-in forms, you attract and capture subscribers. By segmenting your list and using automation tools, you can send targeted emails that resonate with your audience, fostering meaningful connections. Remember, email marketing remains a powerful tool in your marketing arsenal, capable of delivering impressive results in terms of engagement, conversions, and overall business growth.

**Case Study: How a Book Took John's Consulting Business Nationwide** (This story is a fictional example for illustrative purposes)

John Davis started his human resources consulting firm in 2011 after gaining over 15 years of experience in HR leadership roles. He built up a steady client base in his local market providing HR strategy and training services to small businesses.

However, after a few years John's annual revenue plateaued around $220,000. He wanted to expand his reach and help even more companies optimize their HR practices.

In 2018, John wrote a book sharing his insights and expertise from consulting with hundreds of clients. It was titled "People First: An HR Guide to Building Your Best Team."

John self-published the book and promoted it through social media ads, speaking engagements, and business podcast interviews. He offered free digital copies in exchange for email sign-ups.

Within 8 months, John's book had sold over 8,000 copies. Dozens of national magazines and websites featured him as a human resources expert. The book expanded awareness of John's consulting services nationwide.

By positioning himself as a thought leader through the book, John landed major new clients across the country. His annual revenue grew to over $850,000 within a year.

Writing a book detailing his HR insights let John scale his business dramatically. Sharing his knowledge and passion drove exponential growth. The book opened up new opportunities to provide value to companies across the nation.

∾

**In John's words:**

When I started my HR consulting firm back in 2011, I was thrilled to work directly with local small businesses to help improve their people management strategies. However, after a few years I realized I had tapped out the market in my region and wanted to expand my reach across the country.

That's when I wrote a book to prove myself to be a thought leader in my field. While self-publishing was a lot of work, it was one of the best business decisions I ever made. Through the process, I learned so much about marketing myself and profiting from my expertise.

First, I realized just how powerful it was to broadcast my passion and knowledge in book form. It opened doors to speaking with national magazines, websites, and podcasts. Within months, I went from a local consultant to a nationwide HR authority.

Another key lesson was using the book as a lead generation tool by giving away free digital copies. This exploded my email list with ideal potential clients. I could then market other offerings to thousands of new contacts.

While writing the book required discipline, I discovered how enjoyable it was to organize and translate my experience into something of value. Marketing gave me a crash course in leveraging social media, search ads, and speaking events to sell my story.

Overall, self-publishing my consulting insights gave me the platform I needed to rapidly scale up my business. But beyond that, it enabled me to share my mission of helping companies put people first in a much bigger way. I'm so glad I took the leap of faith to become an author. The journey was priceless.

**Chapter Summary:**

The chapter emphasizes building a strong personal brand as a self-published author by showcasing your unique voice and style. Using social media platforms like Facebook, Instagram, Twitter, YouTube,

LinkedIn and Goodreads is recommended to connect with your target audience, build relationships, and promote your book.

Tips are provided for effectively engaging with book bloggers and reviewers through compelling pitches, relationship building, and respecting their time.

Creating an eye-catching book cover that aligns with your genre and resonates with your target audience is highlighted as crucial for attracting readers.

Crafting an enticing book description with hooks, unique selling points, emotional appeal, concise text, and a call to action is advised.

Organizing virtual book launches and author events is discussed, noting benefits like expanded reach, flexibility, and accessibility.

Building an email list through lead magnets and optimized opt-in forms enables targeted campaigns for higher engagement.

Overall, the chapter outlines promotional strategies across social media, bloggers, events, email marketing, and visual elements to spread awareness about your self-published book and connect with readers.

**In our next chapter...**

In this chapter, we delve into the multitude of promotional tactics crucial for the success of a self-published author.

The emphasis is placed on building a strong personal brand that show-cases your unique voice and style. Using social media platforms such as Facebook, Instagram, Twitter, LinkedIn, Goodreads, YouTube, and others is highlighted for effective networking and promotion.

We offer detailed guidance for engagement with book bloggers and reviewers, emphasizing relationship nurturing, intriguing pitches, and time management.

Aesthetic elements like a captivating book cover and a compelling book description are underscored, highlighting their vital roles in piquing reader interest.

The chapter explores the benefits of virtual author events and book launches, focusing on their extended reach, flexibility, and accessibility.

The significance of efficient email marketing and list building are discussed, with insights on lead magnets and opt-in forms for higher engagement.

The chapter explores partnerships with influencers, the role of online advertising and the importance of tracking and analyzing marketing results.

This comprehensive overview serves as a strategic guide to expanding awareness, fostering connections with readers, and ultimately, boosting book sales.

## CHAPTER TEN

# LEVERAGING SOCIAL MEDIA, HARNESSING THE POWER OF INFLUENCERS AND ONLINE PLATFORMS TO BOOST BOOK SALES & EXPAND REACH

USING **Social Media Platforms to Create a Strong Online Presence and Promote Your Self-Published Book Effectively:**

In today's digital age, social media platforms have become powerful tools for individuals and businesses to connect with others, share information, and market products. For self-published authors, harnessing the power of social media can significantly enhance their online presence and effectively promote their books. Here are strategies to use different social media platforms for successful book promotion:

**Facebook:** Create an author page for yourself and share content related to your book regularly. Engage with your followers by organizing giveaways, sharing behind-the-scenes insights into your writing process, or hosting live Q&A sessions. Collaborate with book clubs or groups specific to your book's genre to reach a wider audience and encourage discussions around your work.

**Instagram:** Use visually appealing images and videos to promote your book's cover, teasers, or excerpts. Leverage hashtags relevant to your book and engage with your audience by responding to comments and direct messages. Consider collaborating with popular bookstagrammers or influencers in your genre for features or giveaways, increasing your reach to their followers.

**X aka Twitter:** Use Twitter to share bite-sized updates about your book, upcoming events, or any news related to your writing journey. Engage in conversations with other authors, literary agents, or publishing industry professionals to expand your network. Participate in book-related Twitter chats or use trending hashtags to generate more visibility for your book.

**LinkedIn:** Although primarily a professional networking platform, LinkedIn can still be valuable for authors. Share updates about your book's progress or any relevant articles you come across. Connect with professionals in the publishing industry, agents, or potential readers who share similar interests. Engage in conversations related to writing, publishing, or your book's genre in relevant groups.

Remember, consistency is key across all platforms. Regularly update your social media accounts and provide valuable content to attract and retain followers. Interact with your audience by responding to comments, likes, and shares to build a strong and loyal community around your book.

Using social media platforms effectively can help you create a powerful online presence, connect with readers, and boost your book's visibility. Embrace the opportunities social media offers, and watch your self-published book thrive in the digital world.

**Engaging With Your Target Audience:**

Engaging with your target audience is a crucial step in successfully promoting your book and generating interest among potential buyers. Social media platforms offer an excellent opportunity to connect and interact with your readers in a meaningful way. Here are strategies to build a loyal following and captivate your audience on social media.

**Know your target audience:** Before diving into social media, it's essential to understand who your ideal readers and potential buyers are.

Identify their interests, demographics, and preferred social media platforms. This knowledge will help you tailor your content to resonate with them effectively.

**Create valuable content:** Social media users are bombarded with countless messages daily, so it's essential to provide valuable content that attracts and engages your target audience. Share snippets of your book, behind-the-scenes stories, tips, and insights related to your book's theme. By consistently delivering high-quality content, you can prove yourself to be a credible and knowledgeable author.

**Encourage interaction:** One of the primary goals of engaging with your target audience on social media is to foster meaningful conversations. Encourage your readers to leave comments, ask questions, or share their thoughts about your book. Respond promptly and personally to each comment, showing your audience that you value their input. This interaction will not only deepen the connection with your audience but also create a sense of community around your book.

**Run contests and giveaways:** People love freebies, so running contests or giveaways is a fantastic way to generate interest and excitement about your book. Create simple contests that require participants to engage with your content, such as sharing a particular post or tagging a friend. Offer book-related merchandise, signed copies, or exclusive content as prizes to incentivize participation.

**Use multimedia content:** Social media platforms are highly visual, so utilize multimedia content to make your posts stand out. Share visually appealing images, graphics, or videos related to your book, such as book trailers, author interviews, or behind-the-scenes footage. This will capture the attention of your target audience and make your posts more shareable.

**Collaborate with influencers:** Collaborating with influencers or bloggers with a significant following in your book's niche can amplify your reach and introduce your work to new audiences. Reach out to influencers who align with your book's theme and propose collaborations, such as guest blogging, joint giveaways, or even influencer endorsements. Their endorsement can carry substantial weight and gain attention from potential buyers.

**Engage in conversations:** Social media is not just a platform for self-promotion but an opportunity to engage in relevant conversations within your book's niche. Join relevant groups, participate in conversations, and share your thoughts or insights. This will help you prove yourself to be an authoritative figure in the field, further boosting your credibility.

Consistency is key when engaging with your target audience through social media. Regularly post content, reply to comments, and participate actively in conversations. By building a loyal following and generating interest in your book through meaningful interactions, you can increase your chances of success in the competitive book market.

**Creating Compelling Content to Drive Book Sales:**

Creating compelling content is essential in today's digital age, especially for authors looking to drive book sales and engage with their target audience. By using strategies that captivate readers and resonate with them, authors can increase their visibility, build a loyal fan base, and ultimately drive more sales. Here are strategies to help you create engaging and shareable content:

Research their demographics, interests, and preferences. This will let you tailor your content to their needs and desires, increasing its appeal and shareability. Craft captivating headlines: Your title or headline is the first impression readers will have of your content. Create headlines that are attention-grabbing, intriguing, and promise value. Use strong action words and trigger emotions that will make readers want to click and share.

**Tell compelling stories:** Stories have a powerful impact on readers. Use storytelling techniques to weave narratives that captivate your audience. Share personal anecdotes, experiences, or lessons learned that relate to your book's themes. Stories are relatable, memorable, and encourage readers to share their own experiences.

**Offer valuable insights or knowledge:** Create content that educates or informs your audience. Share valuable insights, tips, or industry knowledge that align with your book's subject matter. Providing useful information not only positions you as an expert but also encourages readers to share your content with others seeking similar information.

**Use multimedia elements:** Enhance your content by incorporating multimedia elements such as images, videos, or infographics. Visuals make your content more visually appealing and increase shareability on social media platforms. Additionally, videos or podcasts can provide an alternative medium for sharing content and engaging with your target audience.

**Encourage user-generated content:** Involve your audience in the content creation process by encouraging them to share their thoughts, reviews, or experiences related to your book. This user-generated content not only adds credibility but also fosters a sense of community. Acknowledge and share this content to show your appreciation for your audience's engagement.

**Optimize for search engines:** To ensure your content reaches a wider audience, optimize it for search engines. Conduct keyword research to identify relevant phrases and incorporate them naturally into your content. This will help your content rank higher in search engine results, increasing its visibility and shareability.

**Engage with your audience:** Foster a two-way conversation with your audience by responding to comments, messages, and reviews. Engaging with your readers not only builds trust and loyalty but also encourages them to share your content with their networks.

**Share on social media and other platforms:** Promote and share your content on various platforms where your target audience spends their time. Use social media platforms like Facebook, Instagram, Twitter, and LinkedIn to reach a broader audience and encourage sharing. Consider collaborating with influencers or partnering with relevant websites or blogs to expand your reach even further.

**Analyze and adapt:** Monitor the performance of your content by tracking metrics such as click-through rates, shares, and engagement. Identify what types of content are resonating the most with your audience and adjust your strategy. Continuously innovating and adapting your content creation strategies will help you stay relevant and drive book sales effectively.

By implementing these strategies, you can create compelling and shareable content that resonates with your target audience, strengthens your brand, and ultimately drives book sales. Remember to stay authentic, provide value, and consistently engage with your audience to build a loyal following that will continue to support your work.

**Leveraging Online Book Communities and Groups:**

When promoting a book online, leveraging book communities, forums, and groups can be an effective strategy to connect with potential readers. Here are some of the online platforms where you can promote your book and engage with like-minded readers:

**Goodreads:** This is one of the largest online communities for readers and authors. Create an author profile, list your book, engage in discussions, participate in reading challenges, and join genre-specific groups to connect with readers interested in your genre.

**Reddit:** Reddit has many book-related subreddits such as r/books, r/suggestmeabook, and genre-specific ones like r/sciencefictionbooks. Engage in discussions, share promotional posts occasionally, and recommend your book when relevant to the conversation. However, remember to be an active member of the community and not just self-promote.

**Facebook Groups:** Join book-related Facebook groups with active members who share similar interests as your target audience. Engage thoughtfully by participating in discussions or starting topics related to your book's genre or themes. Once you establish your presence, you can occasionally promote your book or share updates.

**Twitter Chats:** Participate in book-related Twitter chats, such as #bookishchat or genre-specific ones, where readers discuss their favorite books, authors, and writing. Engage with participants and share insights or recommendations related to your book.

**Online Book Clubs:** Join online book clubs like Oprah's Book Club, Reese's Book Club, or genre-specific book clubs like CrimeReads or Fantasy Book Club. Engage with the community, share your thoughts on selected books, and occasionally promote your own work if it aligns with the club's interests.

**Online Writing Communities:** Platforms like Wattpad, Scribophile, or Authonomy can be perfect for connecting with fellow writers and readers. Share snippets of your book, engage in critiques, and create connections that can lead to readership opportunities.

**Book Blogs:** Search for book bloggers who review books in your genre. Contact them with a personalized message, offering a copy of your book for an honest review. If they enjoy it, they might feature it on their blog, thus reaching their audience of dedicated readers.

Remember, your approach should be focused on genuine connections and meaningful engagement. Avoid excessive self-promotion and take the time to understand the rules and dynamics of each community or group before participating. By leveraging these online book communities and groups, you can increase your book's visibility and connect with readers interested in your work.

### Collaborating With Influencers and Bloggers To Boost Your Book's Visibility And Sales:

Partnering with influencers and bloggers has become an effective strategy for authors and publishers to boost book visibility and sales in today's digital marketing landscape. Influencer marketing refers to leveraging the popularity and large following of influential individuals to promote your product or brand. With the rise of social media, influencers and bloggers have gained significant authority and influence over their audiences, making it a highly effective marketing strategy.

One of the key advantages of collaborating with influencers and bloggers is the sheer reach they have. With thousands or even millions of followers, these individuals have built a loyal audience who trust and value their opinions and recommendations. By partnering with the right influencers who align with the target audience of your book, you can tap into their existing fan base and reach many potential readers who may have not been aware of your book otherwise.

Additionally, collaborating with influencers and bloggers lets you tap into their knowledge and credibility. Influencers are known for their knowledge and specialization in specific niche areas, and their recommendations carry weight with their followers. When an influencer promotes your book, their audience is more likely to view it as a genuine endorsement rather than a direct advertisement. This can significantly increase the chances of their followers being interested in buying your book.

Influencer marketing provides you with the opportunity to create engaging and authentic content. Influencers and bloggers know their audience well and understand how to connect with them effectively. By partnering with them, you can create content tailored to their unique style and preferences, which ultimately makes it more relatable and engaging. Whether it's through reviews, giveaways, sponsored posts, or collaborations, influencer marketing allows you to showcase your book in a way that resonates with the influencer's audience.

In addition to boosting visibility and sales, collaborating with influencers and bloggers can also generate valuable social proof for your book. When an influential blogger or social media personality endorses your book, it adds credibility and confirms its quality in the eyes of potential readers. This social proof can influence the purchasing decisions of their followers and encourage them to give your book a chance.

To get started with influencer marketing, it's important to first identify influencers and bloggers who align with your book's genre, topic, or target audience. Conduct thorough research to ensure their content and values match your brand and goals. Once you've identified potential collaborators, contact them with a personalized and tailored pitch, highlighting why your book would interest their audience.

Collaborating with influencers and bloggers can have a significant impact on the visibility and sales of your book. Leveraging their reach, credibility, and engagement can help you tap into new audiences, generate social proof, and create valuable endorsements. Invest time in identifying the right influencers and creating engaging and authentic content together, and you'll be well on your way to boosting your book's success in the digital age.

### Running Effective Online Advertising Campaigns to Reach A Wider Audience, Increase Book Visibility, And Drive Sales:

Online advertising has become an essential tool for businesses and individuals to promote their products or services. With the rise of digital platforms such as Google Ads, Facebook Ads, and Amazon Ads, it has become easier to reach a wider audience, increase visibility, and drive sales. However, running effective online advertising campaigns requires a strategic approach. Here are tips to help you leverage these advertising platforms effectively:

**Define your goals:** Before diving into online advertising, it is crucial to define your goals. Are you looking to increase brand awareness, drive sales, or promote a specific product? Having clear goals will enable you to create a focused and targeted advertising campaign.

**Understand your target audience:** Knowing your target audience is key to running successful campaigns. Research their demographics, interests, and online behavior to tailor your ads. Facebook Ads, for example, offers detailed targeting options based on location, age, interests, and more.

**Choose the right advertising platform:** Google Ads, Facebook Ads, and Amazon Ads each have distinct features and advantages. Google Ads is great for reaching users searching for your product or service, Facebook Ads enables precise audience targeting, and Amazon Ads targets users with high purchase intent. Consider which platform aligns best with your goals and target audience.

**Craft compelling ad content:** Compelling ad content that resonates with your target audience is crucial. Use attention-grabbing headlines, persuasive copy, and eye-catching visuals to engage users. Experiment with different ad formats such as text, image, video, or carousel ads to see what works best for your campaign.

**Optimize for relevancy and keywords:** In Google Ads, relevance is key. Use relevant keywords in your ad copy, landing page, and URL to improve your Quality Score and ad rank. Incorporate ad extensions such as sitelinks, callouts, and structured snippets to enhance your ad's visibility and click-through rate.

**Track and analyze your campaign:** Regularly track the performance of your ads, adjusting and optimizing as necessary. Use the data provided by the advertising platforms to understand which ads are performing well and which need improvement. This data will help you make informed decisions and improve the effectiveness of your campaigns.

**Set a budget and bidding strategy:** Online advertising lets you set a daily or monthly budget, ensuring you have control over your spending. Additionally, consider your bidding strategy to optimize your ad placement and maximize your return on investment. Use bidding strategies such as cost-per-click (CPC), cost-per-impression (CPM), or cost-per-acquisition (CPA) based on your goals.

**Test and iterate:** Every campaign is an opportunity to learn and improve. Test different ad variations, targeting options, and messaging to identify what resonates best with your audience. Continuously analyze your data and iterate on your strategies to drive better results.

By leveraging online advertising platforms effectively, you can reach a wider audience, increase book visibility, and ultimately drive sales. Remember to set clear goals, understand your target audience, craft compelling content, track your campaign's performance, and continuously iterate to optimize your online advertising efforts.

**Tracking And Analyzing Results:**

. . .

Tracking and analyzing results is an essential step in the marketing process to measure the success of your efforts and make data-driven decisions. By implementing tracking mechanisms, such as website analytics and social media insights, you can gather valuable data that will help you continuously improve your marketing strategies for better book sales. Here are steps to effectively track and analyze your marketing results:

**Set clear goals:** Before you start tracking, define specific goals for your marketing efforts. For example, you might aim to increase website visitors, boost social media engagement, or generate more book sales. Having clearly defined goals will let you measure success accurately.

**Start website analytics:** Use tools like Google Analytics to measure metrics such as website traffic, page views, bounce rate, and conversion rates. By tracking these metrics, you can understand how users are interacting with your website and identify areas for improvement.

**Track social media insights:** Each social media platform provides its own insights or analytics dashboard. Track metrics like follower growth, engagement rate, post reach, and link clicks. Additionally, consider using social media listening tools to analyze sentiment, track conversations, and understand your audience better.

**Use UTM (Urchin Tracking Module) parameters:** If you are running various marketing campaigns across different channels, make use of UTM parameters. These tags can be added to your URLs, letting you track the specific sources of traffic in your website analytics tools. This helps you identify which campaigns and channels are bringing in the most visitors.

**Analyze conversion metrics:** With the help of website analytics, analyze conversion metrics like click-through rates, checkout rates, and sales conversions. These metrics will highlight the effectiveness of your marketing campaigns in driving book sales, enabling you to make data-driven decisions about how to best give your marketing resources.

**A/B testing:** Experiment with different marketing strategies, such as landing page designs, ad copy, or email subject lines, by conducting A/B tests. By comparing the performance of different variations, you can determine which strategies are most effective in driving sales and improving your marketing efforts.

**Regularly review and adapt:** Continuously review your marketing data and insights to identify patterns, trends, and areas for improvement. Keep an eye on new marketing techniques and industry trends to stay updated and adjust your strategies.

**Outline key takeaways:** Document your findings and key takeaways from the tracking and analysis process. These insights will inform your future marketing strategies and help you continuously improve your efforts to drive better book sales.

By implementing these tracking mechanisms and analyzing the results, you can gain valuable insights into the success of your marketing efforts. Use this data to make data-driven decisions and continuously improve your marketing strategies for better book sales.

**Chapter Summary:**

The chapter discusses using social media platforms like Facebook, Instagram, Twitter, LinkedIn, and Goodreads to create a strong online presence and promote your self-published book.

Tips are provided for engaging your target audience through valuable content, interactions, contests, multimedia, and influencer collaborations.

Crafting compelling content with headlines, stories, insights, visuals, user engagement, and optimization is highlighted to captivate readers and drive sales. Leveraging online book communities on platforms like Goodreads, Reddit, Facebook, Twitter, and Wattpad connects authors with potential readers.

Partnering with influencers and bloggers through relationships, content creation, events, and recommendations taps into their existing audiences. Running online advertising campaigns on Google, Facebook, and Amazon requires defined goals, target audience knowledge, optimized and tested content.

Tracking and analyzing marketing results using metrics, analytics, A/B testing, and data review provides insights to refine strategies.

Overall, the chapter outlines promotional tactics across social media, communities, influencers, advertising, and analytics to expand reach and visibility leading to increased book sales.

**In our next chapter...**

This chapter offers a comprehensive guide to marketing strategies vital for the success of a self-published author.

We discuss the importance of creating a robust personal brand and leveraging different social media platforms for promotion and networking.

Practical tips for engaging with book bloggers and reviewers, building relationships, and managing time are provided.

The chapter underlines the significance of appealing visual elements like book covers and persuasive book descriptions in attracting readers.

It also explores the advantages of virtual author events and book launches, emphasizing their extended reach and accessibility.

Discussing email marketing, the chapter enlightens readers on building and segmenting an email list, crafting compelling newsletters, automating sequences, and leveraging data for optimization.

The power of partnerships with influencers, online advertising, and the need for tracking and analyzing marketing results are also discussed.

The chapter serves as a strategic roadmap for authors to broaden their reach, connect with potential readers, and increase book sales through well-planned and executed marketing strategies.

SHARE WHAT YOU KNOW:

## CHAPTER ELEVEN

# USING EMAIL MARKETING AND NEWSLETTER CAMPAIGNS TO EXPAND REACH & BOOK PROMOTION

### THE POWER OF EMAIL MARKETING:

Email marketing has emerged as a powerful tool for businesses to expand their reach and promote their products or services to a wider audience. In this chapter, we will delve into the effectiveness of email marketing and explore the reasons it has become a valuable strategy for businesses of all sizes.

### Cost-effective and Efficient Reach:

One of the primary reasons email marketing is so effective is its cost-effectiveness and efficiency in reaching a larger audience. Unlike traditional forms of marketing, email campaigns let businesses reach potential customers without incurring a lot of advertising costs. With a few clicks, a single email can be dispatched to thousands, if not millions, of recipients, ensuring extensive reach without exhausting resources.

### Personalized Communication:

Another strength of email marketing lies in its ability to provide personalized communication. By segmenting audience data and tailoring messages businesses can send targeted emails that resonate with specific customer demographics or interests. This personalized touch creates a stronger connection with recipients, leading to higher engagement and conversion rates.

### Building and Nurturing Relationships:

Email marketing serves as an excellent platform for building and nurturing relationships with customers. Through regular communication, businesses can establish trust, educate their audience about their products or services, and provide valuable content that keeps recipients engaged. By staying top-of-mind through well-crafted email campaigns, businesses can increase customer loyalty and generate more repeat purchases.

### Versatile Content Delivery:

Email marketing offers great flexibility in terms of content delivery. Whether businesses want to showcase new products, provide updates, offer exclusive discounts, or share informative articles, emails can be tailored to suit various purposes. With eye-catching designs and compelling content, businesses can capture recipients' attention and drive them to take the desired actions.

### Measurable Results and Optimization:

An essential advantage of email marketing is the ability to measure and analyze campaign performance. With the help of email analytics tools, businesses can track open rates, click-through rates, conversions, and other key metrics. These insights allow for continuous improvement and optimization of future campaigns. By understanding what works and resonates with the audience, businesses can refine their strategies and achieve better results.

The power of email marketing lies in its ability to reach a wider audience, provide personalized communication, build relationships, deliver versatile content, and enable measurable results. With its cost-effectiveness and efficiency, businesses can expand their reach, promote their products or services, and achieve higher engagement and conversion rates. By leveraging the potential of email marketing, businesses can unlock a new level of success in today's competitive landscape.

**Building An Email List to Increase the Number Of Subscribers And Grow The Reach Of Your Email Campaigns:**

**Building an Email List:**

A strong and engaging email list is a powerful tool for any business. Not only does it let you communicate directly with your audience, but it also makes sure your messages reach interested individuals more likely to convert into loyal customers. This section will outline various strategies for building a robust email list, maximizing your reach, and ultimately increasing the effectiveness of your email marketing campaigns.

**Website Sign-ups:** One of the most effective methods to grow your email list is by incorporating sign-up forms on your website. Place these forms strategically on high-traffic pages such as your homepage, blog posts, and landing pages. Offer an incentive, like a free resource or exclusive content, to encourage visitors to subscribe. Make sure the sign-up process is quick and hassle-free to prevent potential subscribers from abandoning the process.

**Lead Magnets:** Offering valuable content in exchange for email addresses is a proven technique for building an email list. Create compelling lead magnets, such as e-books, whitepapers, webinars, or checklists, that provide genuine value to your target audience. Promote these lead magnets on your website, through social media, or paid advertising to attract interested individuals willing to exchange their email addresses for your valuable content.

**Partnerships:** Collaborating with complementary businesses or industry influencers can significantly expand your reach and increase the number of subscribers on your email list. Consider partnering with non-competing businesses or influential figures in your niche and offer to promote their content or products in exchange for them promoting your email list or lead magnet to their audience. This mutually beneficial arrangement can attract new subscribers who are already interested in your niche or industry.

**Pop-up and Slide-in Opt-ins:** While individuals find them intrusive, well-timed pop-up or slide-in opt-in forms can be an effective way to capture email addresses. Start these opt-in forms on specific pages where visitors are likely to engage with your content or show exit intent. Customize the forms to match your website's design and ensure they are easily dismissible to provide a positive user experience.

**Social Media Advertising:** Leverage the power of social media platforms to expand your email list. Create compelling advertisements on platforms like Facebook, Instagram, or LinkedIn, offering promotions, exclusive content, or lead magnets to encourage users to join your email list. Target your advertisements to reach individuals who match your target audience and align with your business goals.

**Engaging Content:** Develop a content marketing strategy that focuses on delivering high-quality and engaging content. When visitors find value in your blog posts, videos, or podcasts, they are more likely to subscribe to your email list for future updates. Incorporate relevant call-to-actions (CTAs) within your content, compelling users to subscribe to stay updated or gain access to exclusive content.

**Referral Programs:** Encourage your existing subscribers to refer their friends, colleagues, or acquaintances to join your email list by starting a referral program. Offer incentives such as discounts, exclusive content, or entry into giveaways for successful referrals. Use referral tracking software to ensure correct attribution, rewarding both the referrer and the new subscriber for their participation.

Remember, building an email list is not just about quantity; it's also about quality. Focus on attracting individuals who are genuinely interested in your business or niche, as this will yield higher open rates, click-through rates, and conversions. Regularly engage with your subscribers and provide valuable content to build trust and establish a long-lasting relationship with your audience.

**Crafting Compelling Newsletters to Maximize Open Rates and Click-Through Rates:**

In today's digital age, newsletters have become a powerful tool for businesses to connect with their target audience. However, creating newsletters that engage readers can be a challenge. This chapter delves into the importance of crafting compelling newsletters that are not only relevant but also captivate the attention of your subscribers. We will explore key elements such as designing attractive templates, writing impactful content, and incorporating appealing visuals to maximize open rates and click-through rates.

### Designing Attractive Templates:

The visual appeal of your newsletter plays a crucial role in attracting readers. This section highlights the importance of designing templates that align with your brand identity while being visually appealing. We will discuss tips for selecting fonts, colors, and layout to create a professional and aesthetically pleasing design. Additionally, we will explore the significance of using responsive design to ensure your newsletter looks great on various devices and screens.

### Writing Impactful Content:

Content is king, and this section focuses on writing impactful content that resonates with your target audience. It emphasizes the need to understand your readers' interests, pain points, and expectations. We will explore effective storytelling techniques, personalization strategies, and keeping the content concise yet informative. We will discuss the importance of creating catchy subject lines that entice readers to open your newsletter.

### Incorporating Appealing Visuals:

Visuals can significantly enhance your newsletter's engagement levels. This section dives into the power of incorporating appealing visuals such as images, videos, infographics, and icons to support your content. We will discuss tactics for sourcing high-quality visuals and optimizing their placement within the newsletter to make them visually appealing and relevant to your message. Additionally, we will explore how to balance text and visuals for better readability.

**Maximizing Open Rates and Click-through Rates:**

All efforts put into crafting a compelling newsletter go in vain if it fails to reach the intended audience. This section reveals tips and tricks to maximize open rates and click-through rates. We will cover strategies like segmentation, A/B testing, and personalization to make sure your newsletters do not end up in the dreaded spam folder. Additionally, we will delve into analyzing data and metrics to improve future campaigns.

Crafting compelling newsletters is a vital part of any successful communication strategy. By designing attractive templates, writing impactful content, and incorporating appealing visuals, you can captivate your target audience, increase open rates, and boost click-through rates. This chapter provides valuable insights and practical tactics to help you create newsletters that resonate with your subscribers, ultimately leading to stronger connections and better business outcomes. So, let's dive in and unlock the full potential of your newsletters!

**Segmenting Your Audience to Effectively Categorize Subscribers for More Personalized and Targeted Campaigns:**

Segmenting your audience is a crucial strategy in email marketing. By grouping your subscribers based on demographics, preferences, or behavior, you can create more personalized and targeted campaigns that yield higher engagement and conversion rates. This section will delve into the benefits of list segmentation and provide guidance on how to effectively categorize your subscribers.

**Increased Relevance:** When you segment your email list, you can tailor your messages to specific groups of subscribers who share similar features or interests. By sending content relevant to their needs, you enhance the chances of your emails resonating with the recipients. This ultimately improves open rates, click-through rates, and conversions.

**Improved Engagement:** By understanding your subscribers better and segmenting them appropriately, you can send emails that speak directly to their needs and desires. This personalized approach fosters stronger engagement, as your messages will pique their interest and make them more likely to read, click, and interact with your emails.

**Higher Conversion Rates:** Targeted and relevant campaigns, made possible through segmentation, directly affect conversion rates. When your emails are tailored to address specific pain points, preferences, or buying behaviors, subscribers are more inclined to make a purchase or take the desired action, resulting in improved conversion rates against your marketing goals.

Now that the benefits of list segmentation are clear, here are pointers on how to effectively categorize your subscribers:

a) **Demographic segmentation:** Divide your subscribers based on factors such as age, gender, location, or occupation. This can help you send content that aligns with their demographics, making your emails more relatable and appealing.

b) **Preference-based segmentation:** Ask your subscribers about their preferences and interests during the sign-up process or through periodic surveys. Categorize them according to their stated preferences, letting you send targeted content that matches their specific needs and wants.

c) **Behavior-based segmentation:** Observe and analyze your subscribers' behavior on your website, such as buy history, browsing patterns, or engagement with earlier emails. Categorize them based on their actions, enabling you to create highly targeted campaigns tailored to their behaviors.

d) **Customer stage segmentation:** Divide your subscribers based on their stage in the customer journey, whether they are new leads, repeat customers, or loyal brand advocates. This segmentation lets you nurture different relationships effectively and provides content that suits their current relationship with your brand.

Segmenting your audience is essential in email marketing because it lets you send personalized, relevant, and targeted campaigns. By understanding your subscribers' demographics, preferences, and behaviors, you can create highly engaging email content that drives higher conversions and builds stronger relationships with your audience.

**Automation And Personalization to Enhance Customer Experiences:**

Automation and personalization are two powerful tools that can greatly enhance the effectiveness of email marketing campaigns. In today's fast-paced digital world, where consumers are bombarded with countless messages every day, businesses must cut through the noise and engage with their audience in a meaningful way.

One of the greatest benefits of using email marketing tools is the ability to automate various parts of a campaign. This includes automating sending emails based on specific triggers or actions, such as a subscriber joining a mailing list or making a purchase. By automating these processes, businesses can save time and effort, letting them focus on other important parts of their marketing strategy.

Automated sequences are a valuable feature offered by many email marketing tools. These sequences let businesses send pre-determined emails to subscribers over a specified period. This can be highly effective in nurturing leads and guiding them through the sales funnel. For example, an e-commerce business may set up an automated sequence to send a welcome email, followed by product recommendations, and finally a discount code to encourage a purchase. By carefully planning and crafting these sequences, businesses can drive engagement and conversions.

Personalization is another key element in successful email marketing campaigns. With the wealth of data today, businesses can tailor their email content to individual subscribers based on their preferences, behaviors, and demographics. By using personalization techniques, such as addressing subscribers by their name or including relevant product recommendations, businesses can create a more personalized and engaging experience for their customers. This not only helps to boost open and click-through rates but also fosters a sense of connection and loyalty with the brand.

To use personalization effectively, it is important for businesses to gather and analyze data about their subscribers. This may include information such as buy history, browsing behavior, or demographic details. By segmenting subscribers into different groups based on these features, businesses can craft highly targeted and relevant content that resonates with their audience.

However, it's crucial to balance automation and personalization. While automation can streamline processes and save time, it should not come at the cost of a personalized touch. Businesses should always strive to maintain a human connection with their subscribers by sometimes reviewing and optimizing their automated sequences and personalization techniques.

Automation and personalization are invaluable tools in email marketing. Using email marketing tools to automate campaigns and incorporating personalization techniques, businesses can enhance customer experiences, drive engagement, and ultimately meet their marketing goals. It is important for businesses to continually explore and start best practices in these areas to stay ahead in the competitive landscape and deliver exceptional results for their email marketing efforts.

### Tracking And Analyzing Campaign Performance to Optimize Future Campaigns:

Tracking and analyzing campaign performance is a vital step in the email marketing process. By tracking key metrics and KPIs, marketers can gain valuable insights into their campaign's effectiveness and make data-driven decisions to optimize future efforts. This section will explore the metrics and KPIs that should be tracked, as well as provide guidance on interpreting the data.

**Open Rate:** The open rate measures the percentage of subscribers who open your email. This metric helps gauge the effectiveness of subject lines, preview text, and sender reputation. A low open rate may show a need for more compelling subject lines or improved segmentation.

**Click-Through Rate (CTR):** The CTR measures the percentage of subscribers who clicked on a link within the email. This metric provides insights into the effectiveness of your call to action and email content. A low CTR may show a need for more engaging content or clearer CTAs.

**Conversion Rate:** The conversion rate measures the percentage of subscribers who took the desired action, such as making a purchase or filling out a form. This metric is critical in evaluating the overall success of your campaign. A low conversion rate may show a need for better targeting or more persuasive content.

**Bounce Rate:** The bounce rate measures the percentage of emails not delivered to the recipients' inboxes. There are two types of bounces: hard bounces (permanent delivery failure) and soft bounces (temporary delivery failure). Tracking bounce rates helps maintain a clean email list and sender reputation.

**Unsubscribe Rate:** The unsubscribe rate measures the percentage of subscribers who opted out of receiving future emails. This metric is essential in understanding the level of engagement and relevance of your content. A high unsubscribe rate may show a need for improved targeting or more focused content.

**Spam Complaint Rate:** The spam complaint rate measures the percentage of recipients who marked your email as spam. A high spam complaint rate suggests issues with email content or targeting. Monitor this metric to maintain a good sender reputation and deliverability.

**Return on Investment (ROI):** ROI measures the profitability and effectiveness of your email marketing campaign. By tracking the revenue generated compared to the overall investment, you can assess the success of your campaign and give resources.

Interpreting the data and making data-driven decisions is crucial for optimizing future campaigns. By analyzing trends and patterns in the metrics mentioned above, you can identify areas of improvement. For example, if the open rate is low, you may test different subject lines or send emails at different times. If the conversion rate is low, you may need to refine your targeting, segment your audience better, or optimize your landing pages.

Continuously tracking and analyzing campaign performance is an ongoing process. By leveraging the insights gained from earlier campaigns and incorporating them into future strategies, you can improve the effectiveness of your email marketing efforts and achieve better results.

**Scaling Up and Integrating Email Marketing Efforts to Expand Reach Further And Generate Sustained Growth:**

Scaling up and integrating email marketing efforts can be an effective way to increase brand visibility, improve customer engagement, and generate sustained growth. By combining email marketing with other channels such as cross-promotion, social media integration, and collaboration opportunities, businesses can maximize their impact and reach a wider audience. Here are strategies to consider:

**Cross-promotion:** Collaborate with other businesses or influencers in your industry to cross-promote each other's email campaigns. This could involve including a mention or advertisement for their email newsletter in your own campaigns, and vice versa. By tapping into each other's email lists, you can reach a larger audience and increase the chances of capturing new subscribers.

**Social media integration:** Integrate your email marketing efforts with social media platforms to expand your reach further. Encourage your email subscribers to follow you on social media by including social media icons and links in your email templates. You can also incentivize them to share your email content on their social media profiles by offering exclusive discounts or valuable content. This way, your email campaigns can benefit from the viral nature of social media and reach a wider audience.

**Collaboration opportunities:** Identify potential partnership or collaboration opportunities with complementary businesses or influencers. By joining forces, you can leverage each other's audience to expand your reach. For example, you can co-host webinars or events, create joint email campaigns, or offer exclusive discounts to each other's subscribers. Collaborating with trusted partners can help build credibility and exposure for your email marketing efforts.

**Personalization and segmentation:** To improve the effectiveness of your email marketing campaigns, take advantage of personalization and segmentation techniques. Segment your email list based on various criteria such as demographics, purchase history, or engagement levels. This lets you tailor your messaging and offers to specific groups, increasing the relevance and engagement of your emails. Personalize email content by addressing subscribers by their names and using dynamic content to display customized product recommendations or offers.

**Automation and optimization:** Use automation tools to streamline and optimize your email marketing efforts. Set up automated email sequences based on specific triggers such as sign-ups, purchases, or abandoned carts. This makes sure subscribers receive the right content at the right time, increasing the chances of conversion. Additionally, continually analyze the performance of your email campaigns using metrics such as open rates, click-through rates, and conversion rates. This data can help you identify areas for improvement and make data-driven decisions to optimize your email marketing efforts.

Scaling up and integrating email marketing efforts with other channels can help businesses expand their reach and generate sustained growth. By starting strategies such as cross-promotion, social media integration, collaboration opportunities, personalization, segmentation, automation, and optimization, businesses can maximize the impact of their email campaigns and engage a wider audience.

**Chapter Summary:**

The chapter discusses the power of email marketing for reaching a wider audience in a cost-effective and efficient manner. It highlights the ability to build relationships, deliver versatile content, and enable optimization through data tracking.

Tips are provided for building an email list through website sign-ups, lead magnets, partnerships, pop-ups, social media ads, engaging content, and referral programs. Crafting compelling newsletters requires attractive templates, impactful content, and visuals to maximize open and click rates. Segmenting your audience by demographics, preferences, or behavior enables more personalized and targeted campaigns.

Automation through sequences and personalization based on data improves customer experiences. Tracking and analyzing performance metrics like open rates and conversion rates gives insights to optimize future efforts.

Scaling up efforts through cross-promotion, social media integration, collaborations, segmentation, automation, and optimization expands reach.

The chapter covers strategies across list building, segmentation, compelling content, automation, optimization, and integration to drive email marketing success.

**In our next chapter...**

The chapter emphasizes the importance of collaboration and networking for self-published entrepreneurs to exchange knowledge, increase visibility, expand readership, access opportunities and resources, and find support.

Strategies are provided for finding collaborators through online communities, conferences, niche authors, book projects, webinars, blog tours, and cross-promotion. Harnessing online platforms and social media by optimizing profiles, sharing valuable content, and engaging in relevant groups expands networking reach.

Joining or creating collaborative communities enables peer learning, accountability, exposure, and access to resources. Tips are given for networking at events, researching professionals, listening, offering help, following up, and building long-term relationships.

Cross-promotion and joint ventures are highlighted as powerful collaboration tools to tap into new markets and audiences.

Overall, the chapter outlines various approaches across online engagement, communities, networking, and structured collaborations for entrepreneurs to build connections and partnerships leading to greater success.

～

## CHAPTER TWELVE

# COLLABORATION AND NETWORKING OPPORTUNITIES FOR SELF-PUBLISHED ENTREPRENEURS

THE IMPORTANCE of Collaboration and Networking for Self-Published Entrepreneurs:

In today's digital age, self-publishing has become an increasingly popular and good choice for entrepreneurs looking to share their knowledge with a wide audience. However, successfully navigating the self-publishing world requires more than writing a great book or creating an informative course. Collaboration and networking play crucial roles in the success and growth of self-published entrepreneurs. Here are reasons why collaboration and networking are essential for self-published entrepreneurs:

**Knowledge and skill exchange:** Collaboration and networking provide opportunities for self-published entrepreneurs to connect with other professionals in their field or related industries. By collaborating with these individuals, entrepreneurs can exchange knowledge, insights, and skills that can enhance their own work. This exchange can lead to improvements in content creation, marketing strategies, and overall business development.

**Increased visibility and credibility:** Collaborating with established authors, industry experts, or influential professionals can significantly boost the visibility and credibility of self-published entrepreneurs. By associating with recognized figures, entrepreneurs gain exposure to wider networks of potential readers or clients. This added visibility can help build trust and legitimacy, increasing the likelihood of attracting customers or gaining media coverage.

**Expanding readership and customer base:** Networking lets self-published entrepreneurs tap into existing communities, groups, or organizations with similar interests or target audiences. By connecting with these communities, entrepreneurs can promote their work to a larger, engaged audience, thus expanding their readership or customer base. Building relationships with like-minded individuals who can support and share their work can lead to increased sales, reviews, and word-of-mouth referrals.

**Access to resources and opportunities:** Collaboration and networking open doors to valuable resources and opportunities that self-published entrepreneurs may not have access to on their own. This includes potential partnerships, joint ventures, speaking engagements, guest blogging opportunities, or even media appearances. Through collaborative efforts and networking, entrepreneurs can gain exposure to new platforms, audiences, and revenue streams that can significantly contribute to their growth and success.

**Support and motivation:** The path of self-publishing can challenge and isolate. Collaboration and networking provide self-published entrepreneurs with a supportive community of like-minded individuals who understand and empathize with their journey. This support system can provide encouragement, motivation, and valuable feedback, helping entrepreneurs overcome obstacles and stay focused on their goals.

Collaboration and networking are essential for self-published entrepreneurs because they help with knowledge exchange, enhance visibility and credibility, expand readership and customer base, provide access to resources and opportunities, and offer support and motivation. By engaging in collaboration and networking efforts, self-published entrepreneurs can unlock new doors, grow their businesses, and ultimately thrive in the competitive world of self-publishing.

**Strategies For Finding and Leveraging Collaboration Opportunities with Other Self-Published Entrepreneurs:**

**Join online communities:** Look for platforms and forums specifically designed for self-published entrepreneurs, such as Facebook groups or LinkedIn groups. Join these communities and actively participate in discussions, offer advice, and share your experiences. Networking with other entrepreneurs will help you find collaborators for joint projects.

**Go to industry conferences and events:** Go to conferences and events related to self-publishing, writing, or entrepreneurship. These gatherings provide an opportunity to meet fellow entrepreneurs face-to-face and establish connections. Be prepared with your elevator pitch and business cards to exchange information with potential collaborators.

**Engage with authors in your niche:** Identify authors in your niche with a similar target audience or complementary skills. Contact them by sending a personalized email or connecting on social media. Express your interest in potentially collaborating on a project or marketing campaign that could help both parties.

**Collaborative book projects:** Consider participating in collaborative book projects, where multiple self-published authors contribute chapters or stories to a single book. These projects not only expose your work to a broader audience but also provide an opportunity to cross-promote and collaborate with other authors.

**Co-host webinars or workshops:** Find self-published entrepreneurs with expertise in complementary areas to yours. Collaborate on hosting webinars or workshops that combine your knowledge and skills. This not only expands your reach but also provides valuable content to your audience.

**Participate in blog tours:** Arrange blog tours with other self-published entrepreneurs willing to promote your work on their blogs or social media channels. In return, offer to promote their work on your platforms. This reciprocal arrangement helps both parties reach a wider audience and gain more exposure.

**Create cross-promotion campaigns:** Collaborate with other self-published entrepreneurs to create cross-promotion campaigns. This could involve jointly promoting each other's products or offering bundled packages to your respective audiences. By leveraging each other's networks, you can increase visibility and attract new customers.

**Guest blog or podcast appearances:** Look for opportunities to be a guest on other entrepreneurs' blogs or podcasts. This lets you tap into their existing audience and share your insights, experiences, and knowledge. In return, offer to host guest bloggers or podcasters on your platforms to expand the collaboration further.

**Joint marketing efforts:** Pool resources and skills with other self-published entrepreneurs for joint marketing efforts. This could include sharing costs or resources for advertising, email marketing campaigns, or social media promotions. By working together, you can maximize the impact of your marketing efforts.

**Create a mastermind group:** Form a mastermind group with like-minded self-published entrepreneurs willing to share their knowledge, challenges, and successes. Regularly meet to discuss strategies, exchange ideas, and provide support to each other. The collective wisdom and accountability within the group can lead to valuable collaborations.

**Harnessing the Power of Online Platforms and Social Media to Expand Networking Opportunities:**

In today's digital era, online platforms and social media have transformed the way we connect and communicate with others. These platforms offer immense opportunities for expanding our network and fostering meaningful connections in various personal and professional spheres. Harnessing the power of online platforms and social media can significantly enhance networking opportunities and open doors to new possibilities. Here are key strategies to consider:

**Identify the Right Platforms:** Begin by identifying the online platforms and social media networks that align with your interests, goals, and target audience. LinkedIn, Twitter, Facebook, Instagram, and professional community websites are popular choices, but select the ones that cater specifically to your industry or niche.

**Optimize Your Profiles:** Craft an engaging and professional profile that highlights your skills, experiences, and goals. Use keywords and relevant hashtags to enhance visibility. It is essential to present yourself authentically and brand yourself effectively to attract the right connections.

**Join Relevant Groups and Communities:** Participate actively in industry-specific or interest-based groups on platforms like LinkedIn and Facebook. Engage in discussions, contribute valuable insights, and connect with like-minded individuals who share similar interests and can become valuable connections.

**Create and Share Valuable Content:** Establish yourself as a thought leader or expert in your field by creating and sharing valuable content. These may include industry insights, informative articles, blog posts, or video tutorials. Consistently creating and sharing valuable content helps to build your credibility and attract a wider network of professionals.

**Engage with Your Network:** Actively engage with your existing network by commenting, liking, and sharing their content. This interaction shows your support and fosters a stronger connection. Additionally, attending webinars, virtual conferences, and participating in online networking events can also help with new connections.

**Use Advanced Search Functions:** Many online platforms have advanced search functions that let you find and connect with individuals based on specific criteria such as location, industry, or job title. Use these functions to identify potential networking contacts and send them personalized, thoughtful connection requests.

**Provide Value to Others:** Networking is a two-way street. Look for ways to contribute and provide value to your connections. This may involve offering advice, sharing resources, or making introductions. By being helpful and generous, you build a reputation as a valuable connection, making others more likely to reciprocate and help you in return.

**Leverage Social Media Advertising:** Consider using social media advertising to target specific audiences or industries. This can help you expand your reach, attract more connections, and increase your networking opportunities.

By harnessing the power of online platforms and social media, you can expand networking opportunities exponentially. Remember, networking is about building and nurturing authentic relationships. Be genuine, strategic, and consistent in your efforts, and you'll discover a vast array of connections that can help both your personal and professional growth.

### The Benefits of Joining or Creating Collaborative Communities and Groups For Self-Published Entrepreneurs:

The benefits of joining or creating collaborative communities and groups for self-published entrepreneurs are numerous and can greatly contribute to business growth and personal development. Here are some of the key advantages:

**Networking opportunities:** Collaborative communities and groups provide access to a network of like-minded individuals who share similar goals and aspirations. Building relationships with other self-published entrepreneurs can lead to valuable partnerships, collaborations, and referrals. Networking within these communities can open doors to new opportunities and expand your reach in the industry.

**Peer learning and knowledge exchange:** Being part of a collaborative community allows for the exchange of ideas, strategies, and best practices. Entrepreneurs can learn from the experiences of others, gaining insights into successful self-publishing methods, marketing techniques, and business growth strategies. This collective wisdom can accelerate personal and professional growth, enabling entrepreneurs to identify potential pitfalls and avoid common mistakes.

**Support and accountability:** Self-publishing can sometimes be a solitary journey, but being part of a collaborative community brings a sense of support and camaraderie. Members can provide encouragement during tough times, offer constructive feedback, answer questions, and share resources. The sense of accountability within the group motivates entrepreneurs to set and achieve goals, keeping them focused and on track.

**Increased visibility and exposure:** By engaging with collaborative communities, entrepreneurs can enhance their visibility within their niche. Sharing knowledge, participating in discussions, and contributing valuable content within these groups can establish credibility and position oneself as an expert. This increased exposure can lead to wider recognition, more opportunities for guest blogging, speaking engagements, media coverage, and ultimately, increased sales and revenue.

**Access to resources and collective knowledge:** Collaborative communities often offer an array of resources and expert advice that may otherwise be challenging to access. Entrepreneurs can tap into the collective knowledge of the group to overcome obstacles, gain feedback on their work-in-progress, or seek recommendations for professional services like editors, cover designers, or book marketers. Additionally, communities often organize training sessions, webinars, and workshops to further enhance skills and knowledge.

**Motivation and inspiration:** Being surrounded by other self-published entrepreneurs who are driven and ambitious can have a profound impact on one's own motivation and inspiration. Sharing success stories, celebrating achievements, and seeing the accomplishments of peers can fuel determination and encourage entrepreneurs to push their own boundaries. Emotional support and sense of belonging can boost confidence, ultimately leading to greater resilience in the face of challenges.

Overall, joining or creating collaborative communities and groups for self-published entrepreneurs can provide a supportive environment, foster learning, and growth, expand networks, boost visibility, and offer access to valuable resources. These collective efforts contribute to the overall success and sustainability of self-published businesses.

**Tips For Effectively Networking and Building Mutually Beneficial Relationships with Industry Professionals:**

**Go to industry events:** Attend conferences, seminars, and workshops related to your field. These events provide excellent opportunities to meet industry professionals and build relationships.

**Be proactive:** Don't wait for others to approach you. Introduce yourself and strike up conversations with industry professionals. Be confident, approachable, and keep the conversation focused on their knowledge and experiences.

**Research and prepare:** Before attending any networking event, research the professionals you expect to meet. Learn about their background, achievements, and current projects. This will help you engage them in meaningful conversations and show your interest and knowledge in their work.

**Be genuine and authentic:** Building relationships is about showing genuine connections. Be yourself and show sincere interest in others' work and accomplishments. Avoid sounding too scripted or rehearsed; instead, focus on building a rapport by engaging in open and honest conversations.

**Be a good listener:** Networking is not just about talking about yourself; it's equally important to listen attentively to others. Pay close attention to what industry professionals are saying, ask relevant follow-up questions, and show genuine interest in their perspectives. This will leave a positive impression and make them more likely to remember you.

**Offer help and support:** Look for opportunities to help others. If you have any skills, knowledge, or resources that can help industry professionals, offer your assistance with no expectations. Providing value to others builds trust and fosters stronger relationships.

**Follow up after networking events:** After meeting industry professionals, follow up with a personalized email or LinkedIn message. Thank them for their time, express your appreciation for their insights, and mention any specific points from your conversation. This gesture keeps the conversation going and helps solidify your connection.

**Maintain regular contact:** Building relationships is an ongoing effort. Stay in touch with industry professionals by sharing relevant articles, thought-provoking insights, or congratulating them on their achievements. Regularly reaching out fosters a mutually beneficial relationship and makes sure you stay on their radar.

**Attend industry-specific online communities or forums:** Participate in online communities, such as LinkedIn groups or industry-specific forums, where professionals share knowledge and discuss industry trends. Contribute insightful comments and engage in meaningful discussions to establish your knowledge and expand your network.

**Be patient and persistent:** Building strong professional relationships takes time. It is essential to be patient and persistent while networking. Keep nurturing your connections, show your dedication, and stay engaged in the industry. Over time, mutually beneficial relationships will naturally evolve.

### Exploring Cross-Promotion and Joint Ventures as Powerful Collaboration Tools for Self-Published Entrepreneurs:

In today's highly competitive entrepreneurial landscape, self-published entrepreneurs are constantly seeking innovative strategies to expand their reach and maximize their success. Two powerful collaboration tools that have emerged as effective methods are cross-promotion and joint ventures. By exploring cross-promotion and joint ventures, self-published entrepreneurs can significantly enhance their brand exposure, tap into new markets, and ultimately increase their revenue streams.

Cross-promotion involves partnering with another entrepreneur or business to promote each other's products or services. It enables self-published entrepreneurs to tap into a wider audience by leveraging the existing customer base of their partner. For example, a self-published author specializing in personal development books could collaborate with a wellness coach or motivational speaker who shares a similar target audience. By mutually promoting each other's work through social media posts, email newsletters, or guest blog posts, both entrepreneurs can benefit from increased exposure to a highly relevant and engaged audience.

In addition to cross-promotion, joint ventures provide self-published entrepreneurs with an opportunity to pool resources and combine forces with another entrepreneur or business to achieve common goals. Joint ventures involve creating a new entity or project that benefits both parties involved. For example, a self-published entrepreneur who specializes in creating online courses could team up with a web developer to create a comprehensive e-learning platform. By sharing knowledge, resources, and marketing efforts, both entrepreneurs can create a powerful product offering that attracts a wider customer base and generates higher revenue.

The benefits of exploring cross-promotion and joint ventures for self-published entrepreneurs are numerous. First, both strategies provide access to a broader audience without the need for extensive advertising budgets. By partnering with already-established entrepreneurs or businesses, self-published entrepreneurs can tap into their partner's credibility and reputation, gaining the trust of potential customers more easily. This can result in increased sales and a faster growth trajectory for their business.

Second, cross-promotion and joint ventures let self-published entrepreneurs diversify their offerings or enter new markets. Collaborating with complementary entrepreneurs or businesses enables them to expand their product line or reach a different demographic, thus opening new revenue streams. This diversification can help mitigate risks and ensure sustainability in the long term.

Last, cross-promotion and joint ventures foster valuable networking opportunities. By building relationships and collaborating with like-minded entrepreneurs, self-published entrepreneurs can gain valuable insights, share experiences, and support one another in navigating the entrepreneurial journey. Networking with prominent figures in the industry can also lead to future collaboration opportunities and increased visibility within the entrepreneurial community.

Cross-promotion and joint ventures have emerged as powerful collaboration tools for self-published entrepreneurs. Through cross-promotion, entrepreneurs can leverage each other's customer base to expand their reach and increase brand exposure. Joint ventures allow for resource sharing and the creation of new, mutually beneficial projects. By embracing these collaboration tools, self-published entrepreneurs can enhance their chances of success, diversify their offerings, and foster valuable partnerships within their industry.

**Chapter Summary:**

The chapter emphasizes the importance of collaboration and networking for self-published entrepreneurs to exchange knowledge, increase visibility, expand readership, access opportunities and resources, and find support.

Strategies are provided for finding collaborators through online communities, conferences, niche authors, book projects, webinars, blog tours, and cross-promotion. Harnessing online platforms and social media by optimizing profiles, sharing valuable content, and engaging in relevant groups expands networking reach.

Joining or creating collaborative communities enables peer learning, accountability, exposure, and access to resources. Tips are given for networking at events, researching professionals, listening, offering help, following up, and building long-term relationships.

Cross-promotion and joint ventures are highlighted as powerful collaboration tools to tap into new markets and audiences.

Overall, the chapter outlines various approaches across online engagement, communities, networking, and structured collaborations for entrepreneurs to build connections and partnerships leading to greater success.

. . .

**In our next chapter...**

This chapter explores the importance of nurturing relationships with readers for self-published authors.

It emphasizes the power of authenticity, transparency, and relatability in building trust and connection with readers. Strategies such as engaging on social media via live Q&A sessions, exclusive content, and online book clubs are discussed.

The chapter also delves into the significance of email marketing, highlighting how personalized communication and exclusive updates can foster deeper relationships.

The potential of in-person events and book signings for networking and expressing gratitude directly to readers is underlined.

The chapter further underscores the importance of reader feedback and reviews in improving future works and maintaining open dialogue.

Tapping into influencer networks and collaborating with fellow authors for exposure and extended readership is also covered.

The chapter serves as a guide to creating a sense of community among readers, helping with interactions, and transforming readers into brand advocates.

❧

## CHAPTER THIRTEEN

# NURTURING RELATIONSHIPS WITH YOUR READERS AND LEVERAGING BOOK SUCCESS
## BUILDING AUTHENTICITY AND TRUST:

BUILDING authenticity and trust is crucial when connecting with readers. In a world full of information overload and endless options, readers are more likely to engage with content they find relatable and trustworthy. To show this genuine connection, it is important to share personal stories, be transparent, and create a sense of relatability.

Foremost, sharing personal stories can help readers feel a connection to the content and the writer. When writers reveal their vulnerabilities, struggles, and successes, it humanizes them and shows they understand the experiences of their readers. Personal stories provide a unique perspective, letting readers see the writer as someone who has faced similar situations, overcome obstacles, and learned valuable lessons. By sharing personal stories, writers show readers they are not alone in their experiences, fostering a sense of empathy and trust.

Transparency is another key aspect of building authenticity and trust. Readers appreciate honesty and openness in content creators. By acknowledging their biases, limitations, and mistakes, writers show they are not trying to manipulate or deceive readers. Transparency creates an atmosphere of trust, as readers feel assured that the content, they are consuming is genuine and reliable. It also invites readers to engage in a more meaningful way, as they are more likely to feel comfortable sharing their own thoughts and experiences.

Creating a sense of relatability is also essential in building authenticity and trust. Readers are more likely to engage with content that resonates with their own lives and experiences. As writers, it is important to understand and acknowledge the diversity of readers' backgrounds, cultures, and perspectives. By incorporating relatable examples, anecdotes, and references, writers can bridge the gap between themselves and the readers, creating a stronger connection and fostering trust. Relatability encourages readers to feel understood and valued and to invest their time and attention into the content.

Building authenticity and trust with readers requires sharing personal stories, being transparent, and creating a sense of relatability. By sharing personal experiences, writers show empathy and understanding, letting readers feel a connection and trust in the content. Transparency assures readers they are not being deceived or manipulated, creating an atmosphere of authenticity. Finally, creating a sense of relatability helps readers feel understood and encourages them to engage more deeply with the content. Combining these elements can lay the foundation for a genuine and trustworthy relationship between writers and readers.

**Engaging With Readers Through Social Media:**

Engaging with readers through social media has become an essential part of an author's marketing strategy in today's digital age. Using various platforms and techniques, authors can strengthen their connection with their audience and create a loyal fanbase. Here are effective ways authors can interact with their readers through social media:

**Live Q&A Sessions:** Organizing live question and answer sessions lets authors directly interact with their readers. Platforms like Instagram Live, Facebook Live, or YouTube Live enable authors to answer fans' questions in real-time. This not only provides valuable insights into the author's writing process but also allows readers to connect with the author on a more personal level.

**Hosting Giveaways:** Giveaways are a fantastic way to boost engagement and draw attention to an author's work. By running contests on social media platforms, authors can offer signed copies of their books, merchandise related to their work, or even exclusive sneak peeks. This can encourage readers to actively participate, share content, and promote the author's work within their own networks.

**Responding to Comments and Messages:** Engaging with readers on social media involves participating in conversations sparked by comments and direct messages. Responding to comments not only shows appreciation to readers but also encourages others to join the conversation. Additionally, replying to direct messages lets authors establish a more personal connection with individual readers and address their specific queries or concerns.

**Behind-the-Scenes Content:** Sharing behind-the-scenes content provides readers with an exclusive look into an author's creative process. This can include sneak peeks of works in progress, sharing inspirations, or even giving readers a glimpse into the author's workspace. Such content helps readers feel involved and gives them a sense of being part of the author's journey.

**Exclusive Content for Social Media Followers:** Rewarding social media followers with exclusive content can strengthen the bond between authors and readers. This can include releasing excerpts from upcoming books, offering additional short stories or bonus chapters accessible only to followers, or sharing insights into characters or settings that are not found in the published works.

**Online Book Clubs or Read-A longs:** Creating online book clubs or engaging in read-a longs with readers provides a platform for in-depth discussions about books. Authors can set up dedicated hashtags on platforms like Twitter or Instagram, letting readers share their thoughts, quotes, or even fan-art related to the book. This helps with a sense of community and allows authors to join the conversation and gain valuable feedback.

Utilizing social media platforms and techniques can enhance an author's engagement with their readers. By organizing live Q&A

sessions, hosting giveaways, responding to comments and messages, sharing behind-the-scenes content, offering exclusive content, and participating in online book clubs, authors can develop a strong and loyal fanbase, ultimately leading to increased book sales and a more devoted readership.

**Using Email Marketing:**

**Using email marketing:** Building an email list and fostering deeper connections with readers through exclusive content, updates, and personalized communication

Email marketing has long been considered a powerful tool for businesses to engage their audience, promote their products or services, and ultimately drive conversions. By effectively building an email list and starting email marketing strategies, businesses can cultivate meaningful relationships with their readers. This section highlights the benefits of building an email list and using email marketing strategies to foster deeper connections with readers through exclusive content, updates, and personalized communication.

**Building an Email List:**

Building an email list is crucial for businesses as it lets them directly reach out to interested individuals or potential customers who have willingly provided their contact information. By creating opt-in forms on your website, landing pages, or social media platforms, you can easily collect email addresses and build a list of subscribers. This list acts as a pool of engaged readers who have shown interest in your brand and are more likely to be receptive to your email campaigns.

**Exclusive Content:**

One of the primary benefits of email marketing is the ability to offer exclusive content to your subscribers. By providing valuable and unique content such as e-books, guides, or industry insights, you can show your knowledge and establish yourself as a trusted source. Exclusive content gives your readers a reason to stay subscribed and eagerly await your emails. This value-added approach not only increases engagement but also enhances the perception of your brand, leading to better conversion rates in the long run.

**Regular Updates:**

Email marketing lets businesses stay connected with their readers by providing regular updates. Whether its new product launches, upcoming events, discount offers, or informative newsletters, email campaigns enable you to keep your audience informed and engaged. By maintaining consistent communication, you foster a sense of loyalty and trust, making sure your readers remain interested and informed about your brand.

**Personalized Communication:**

Personalization is a key factor in successful email marketing. Use the data collected from your subscribers to personalize your emails, making them more relevant and engaging. Address your readers by their names, segment your email lists based on factors like demographics or purchase history, and tailor your content. This personalized approach makes your readers feel valued and understood, increasing the level of connection and interaction they have with your brand.

**Improved Conversions and Customer Retention:**

By establishing strong connections with your readers through effective email marketing, you enhance the likelihood of conversions and customer retention. A well-crafted email campaign can significantly improve click-through rates, leading to increased website traffic and potential sales. Engaged subscribers are more likely to recommend your brand to others, increasing your customer base through word-of-mouth promotion.

Email marketing is a powerful tool that can deepen connections with readers, resulting in various benefits for businesses. By building an email list, delivering exclusive content, providing regular updates, and personalizing communication, you can foster a strong bond with your readers. This boosts engagement, improves conversion rates, and leads to increased customer loyalty. Starting effective email marketing strategies is essential for businesses aiming to nurture their audience and achieve long-term success.

## Holding Events and Book Signings:

In today's digital age, where most interactions happen virtually, the importance of in-person events, book signings, and speaking engagements for authors cannot be underestimated. These events provide a unique opportunity for authors to directly meet their readers, express gratitude for their support, and establish long-lasting relationships. Let's explore the benefits of holding these events and book signings.

First, in-person events let authors engage with their readers on a personal level. Writing is often a solitary endeavor, and authors rarely get to connect with the individuals who consume their work. Such events provide a platform for authors to have meaningful conversations, exchange ideas, and gain insights into their readers' experiences. By listening to their readers, authors can better understand their preferences, desires, and even receive valuable feedback. This interaction can significantly enrich an author's understanding of their audience, enabling them to refine their writing style and cater to readers' interests in future works.

Second, book signings offer a unique opportunity for authors to thank their readers in person. For many readers, meeting the author of their favorite book or series is a thrilling experience. By attending book signings, authors convey their appreciation for their readers' support, acknowledging their role in the author's success. A genuine expression of gratitude goes a long way in fostering a sense of loyalty and connection between authors and their readers.

Building lasting relationships is a crucial part of an author's career. In-person events provide a platform for authors to create a community around their work. By meeting readers face-to-face, authors can foster a sense of belonging and create a shared experience among their audience. This sense of community encourages readers to become brand ambassadors, spreading the word about the author's work and boosting their visibility.

Speaking engagements allow authors to share their knowledge, insights, and inspiration with a broader audience. Whether it be at literary festivals, conferences, or universities, speaking engagements let authors establish themselves as thought leaders in their respective fields. This visibility not only enhances their reputation but also opens new opportunities, such as collaborations, book deals, and invitations to prestigious events.

In-person events and book signings also provide networking opportunities for authors. They can connect with fellow authors, publishers, agents, and other industry professionals. Building relationships with these individuals can lead to collaborations, mentorship, or even future book deals. Networking lets authors expand their reach, gain exposure to new markets, and learn from the experiences of others.

Holding in-person events, book signings, and speaking engagements is a crucial element for authors seeking to connect with their readers, express gratitude, and create lasting relationships. By engaging with readers on a personal level, authors can gain valuable insights and refine their craft. Expressing gratitude in person strengthens the connection between authors and their readers, fostering loyalty and word-of-mouth recommendations. Finally, these events offer excellent networking opportunities and let authors establish themselves as influential figures in their field. In the era of digital communication, in-person events remain invaluable in creating a bond between authors and their readers, leaving a lasting impact on both parties.

**Leveraging Reader Feedback and Reviews to Improve Future Works, Engage In Open Dialogue, And Show Appreciation For Their Input:**

Readers have evolved from solely consuming literature to becoming active collaborators in the creative process, reflecting the participatory nature of the digital age. Their feedback and reviews hold immense value and can be leveraged to enhance future works, strengthen writer-reader relationships, and foster a vibrant literary community. As writers, it is crucial to actively seek feedback, engage in open dialogue, and show appreciation for the valuable input readers provide.

Foremost, actively seeking feedback from readers shows a commitment to growth and improvement. By inviting readers to share their thoughts and opinions on your work, you open the doors to valuable insight that can help identify strengths and weaknesses. This feedback can refine your writing style, develop compelling characters, and create immersive worlds. Without the input of readers, it becomes challenging to gauge the impact and resonance of your work, making sincere feedback an indispensable tool for growth.

Reviews, particularly those left on public platforms, carry significant weight in shaping public perception. By monitoring and analyzing these reviews, you gain a deeper understanding of how your work is received by readers. Whether positive or negative, reviews hold valuable insights that can guide your future creative endeavors. They may highlight parts that resonated strongly with readers, enabling you to build on those elements in later works. Likewise, constructive criticism can reveal areas that need improvement, providing the opportunity for personal and artistic growth.

Engaging in open dialogue with readers allows for a deeper connection and understanding, creating a sense of community. In today's interconnected world, social media platforms and online forums provide accessible spaces for such interactions. Responding to readers' comments, questions, and concerns fosters a sense of appreciation for their time and effort in sharing feedback. It also encourages ongoing conversations, building a loyal and engaged reader base, and creating a strong bond between the writer and their audience.

Acknowledging and appreciating reader feedback is essential in nurturing a symbiotic relationship. Whether through direct contact or public acknowledgments, expressing gratitude shows you value their input and supports a sense of mutual respect. By incorporating their suggestions and addressing their concerns, you show an openness to collaboration and a willingness to learn from your readership.

Leveraging reader feedback and reviews is vital for writers seeking growth, connection, and improvement. Seeking feedback, engaging in open dialogue, and showing appreciation for their input form the foundation of a strong writer-reader relationship. Embrace constructive criticism, celebrate the praise, and view both as opportunities to refine your craft, create meaningful connections, and ultimately become a better writer.

**Collaborating With Influencers and Fellow Authors to Expand Readership, Gain Exposure, & Tap Into Each Other's Audience:**

Collaborating with influencers, such as social media personalities or bloggers, and co-writing with fellow authors can be highly advantageous for authors and writers. By teaming up with relevant influencers or co-authors, writers can expand their readership, gain exposure, and tap into each other's audiences. Let's explore the benefits of these collaborations:

**Expanded Readership:** Influencers and authors often have a dedicated following, with readers interested in their knowledge or writing style. By collaborating with them, authors can reach a wider audience that may not have been aware of their work before. This expanded readership can lead to increased book sales, fan base growth, and greater overall exposure.

**Exposure to New Markets:** Teaming up with influencers or co-authors can open doors to new markets and demographics. Influencers have their own niche communities that have shown a keen interest in their content. Co-authors may have a different style or background that appeals to a new group of readers. By tapping into these new markets, authors can expand their readership and attract a diverse range of fans.

**Enhanced Credibility:** Collaborating with well-established influencers or successful authors can enhance an author's credibility. Associating one's work with an influencer or co-author who is respected and admired in the industry can lend legitimacy to one's writing. This increased credibility can attract new readers and create opportunities for endorsements, speaking engagements, and other collaborations.

**Network Expansion:** Collaborating with influencers and fellow authors lets writers expand their professional network. Building relationships with influencers and authors who have similar interests or target audiences can lead to new opportunities, such as attending industry events or participating in joint promotional activities. These connections can also provide writers with valuable advice, support, and guidance throughout their careers.

**Cross-Promotion:** Collaborations offer the opportunity for cross-promotion, where influencers and authors promote each other's work to their respective audiences. This mutually beneficial arrangement allows for sharing promotional resources, such as social media mentions, blog features, or guest appearances on podcasts. This cross-promotion can significantly increase an author's exposure, as readers of the influencer or co-author are more likely to trust and explore recommended works.

**Creative Synergy:** Co-writing with fellow authors can result in unique creative synergies. Joining forces with another writer can bring fresh perspectives, ideas, and writing styles to the table. By collaborating on a joint project, authors can leverage each other's strengths, complement each other's weaknesses, and create a compelling story that combines their unique voices. This collaboration can lead to an inspiring and rewarding creative process, as well as a piece of work that resonates with a broader audience.

Collaborating with influencers and fellow authors provides many benefits for writers. From expanded readership and exposure to tapping into new markets and networks, these collaborations can significantly boost an author's career. By teaming up with relevant influencers or co-writing with other authors, writers can enhance their credibility, reach a wider audience, and create exciting and engaging content.

**Creating A Sense of Community to Encourage Readers to Connect With Each Other And Form a Loyal Following:**

Creating a sense of community around your book or brand is crucial for fostering reader engagement and building a loyal following. This can be achieved through various means, such as online forums, author websites, or dedicated social media groups. By helping with connections among readers, you not only encourage them to engage with your content but also create a space where they can interact and share their thoughts with like-minded individuals. Here's why fostering a community is significant:

**Reader Engagement:** A community provides an avenue for readers to actively engage with your book or brand. By participating in discussions, sharing opinions, and asking questions, readers feel a deeper connection to your work. This engagement goes beyond passively consuming content and encourages readers to become active participants in the community you've built.

**Sense of Belonging:** Humans have an innate desire to belong and connect with others who share their interests. By fostering a community, you're providing a space where readers can find like-minded individuals with whom they can discuss their favorite parts of your book or brand. This sense of belonging increases their loyalty and attachment to your work.

**Word-of-Mouth Promotion:** When readers feel a strong connection to your book or brand and are part of a community centered on it, they're more likely to recommend it to others. Positive experiences and fulfilling interactions within the community serve as endorsements, leading to organic word-of-mouth promotion. This recommendation is often more influential than marketing efforts alone.

**Access to Exclusive Content:** Fostering a community lets you reward the loyalty of your readers by providing exclusive content or behind-the-scenes insights. This could include sneak peeks, author Q&A sessions, or special offers. By offering unique benefits to community members, you not only make them feel valued but also encourage them to remain actively involved and promote your book or brand further.

**Feedback and Iteration:** Creating a community provides a platform for direct feedback from readers. This feedback can be immensely valuable for improving your future work or expanding your brand. By listening and engaging with your audience, you can learn about their preferences, gauge their reactions, and continuously iterate and refine your content to better cater to their needs and desires.

Fostering a community around your book or brand is significant as it creates reader engagement, a sense of belonging, and encourages word-of-mouth promotion. It also lets you reward your loyal readers and gain valuable feedback for future improvements. Building and nurturing a community is an investment that fosters a loyal following, ultimately leading to increased readership, sales, and brand growth.

**Chapter Summary:**

The chapter discusses building authenticity and trust with readers by sharing personal stories, being transparent, and creating relatability. Engaging with readers on social media through live Q&A sessions, giveaways, responding to comments, behind-the-scenes content, online book clubs, and exclusive content for followers is highlighted.

Email marketing by building a list, offering exclusive content, providing updates, and personalizing communication fosters deeper connections.

Holding in-person events and book signings enables authors to connect directly with readers, express gratitude, and network.

Leveraging reader feedback and reviews helps improve future works, have open dialogue, and show appreciation. Collaborating with influencers and fellow authors expands readership, gains exposure, and taps into existing audiences.

Creating a sense of community encourages readers to connect with each other, engage more, and become brand advocates.

Overall, the chapter provides strategies for building connections with readers, helping with interactions, expressing gratitude, collaborating with others, and nurturing an engaged community.

**In our next chapter...**

This chapter delves into the crucial parts of strategic pricing that align with profitability goals and target audience needs, discussing pricing models such as cost-plus, value-based, and dynamic pricing.

It investigates the merits and pitfalls of different distribution channels, including online marketplaces like Amazon and Etsy, and the opportunity to engage with customers in physical stores.

The chapter further explores alternate avenues for monetization, suggesting online courses, consulting services, and affiliate marketing as potent ways to leverage digital platforms.

It champions the power of collaborative partnerships in growth, with emphasis on joint marketing, cross-promotion, and resource sharing.

Networking receives significant attention, with the chapter pinpointing conferences, online forums, workshops, and mastermind groups as places to connect with the self-publishing community.

With a nod toward the importance of social media in building credibility and fostering collaborations, the chapter concludes with effective negotiation tactics for sustainable, long-term relationships.

Overall, this chapter serves as a comprehensive guide to maximize profitability in self-publishing.

## CHAPTER FOURTEEN

# MAXIMIZING PROFITABILITY - PRICING, DISTRIBUTION, & MONETIZATION STRATEGIES

IMPORTANCE OF STRATEGIC **Pricing Strategies to Align with Profitability Goals and Target Market Needs:**

**Importance of Strategic Pricing Strategies:**

Pricing is a critical part of any business strategy. It not only determines the revenue generated but also plays a crucial role in shaping consumer perception of the value of products or services. This is especially true for self-published products or services, where the business owner has complete control over pricing decisions. In this context, implementing effective pricing strategies becomes important.

Strategic pricing involves considering various factors such as costs, market demand, competition, and customer preferences to determine the best price point that maximizes profitability while meeting the needs of the target market. Let's discuss common pricing approaches for self-published products or services and understand the importance of aligning pricing decisions with profitability goals and target market needs.

**Cost-Plus Pricing:** This approach involves determining the price by adding a markup percentage to the cost of producing or delivering the product or service. While it ensures cost recovery and provides a base-line for profitability, it may not consider other external factors such as market demand or competition. So using cost-plus pricing alone may lead to under or overpricing, affecting profitability and customer perception.

**Value-Based Pricing:** In this approach, the price is determined based on the perceived value of the product or service to the customers. It considers customer preferences, benefits derived from the product/service, and competitor pricing. By aligning the price with the value perceived by the target market, businesses can charge a premium for superior offerings, differentiate from competition, and optimize profitability.

**Dynamic Pricing:** This pricing approach involves adjusting prices based on real-time market conditions, such as demand, supply, or competitor pricing. It lets businesses adapt to changing circumstances and optimize revenue. For example, a self-published e-book author might price their book lower to attract early buyers, and gradually increase the price as demand grows. Dynamic pricing requires tracking market trends and competition on an ongoing basis.

**Aligning pricing decisions with profitability goals and target market needs is crucial for several reasons:**

**Ideal Revenue Generation:** Pricing directly affects the top line by determining the revenue generated. By analyzing costs, market demand, and customer preferences, businesses can set prices that maximize revenue and contribute to profitability.

**Competitive Advantage:** Effective pricing strategies can help differentiate self-published products or services from competitors. By understanding the value perceived by customers and pricing businesses can create a USP, attracting customers and gaining a competitive edge.

**Target Market Alignment:** Pricing decisions should align with the target market's affordability, willingness to pay, and perceived value. By understanding customer needs and preferences, businesses can develop pricing strategies that cater to their target market, maximizing the chances of sales and customer satisfaction.

**Profitability Sustainability:** Pricing decisions are needed to ensure profitability in the long run. By considering costs, competition, and demand, businesses can avoid underpricing that hampers profitability or overpricing that may deter customers. Pricing should balance generating enough profit margins and attracting customers.

Strategic pricing plays a crucial role in the success of self-published products or services. Businesses must evaluate different pricing approaches, such as cost-plus pricing, value-based pricing, or dynamic pricing, to determine the best price point. Pricing decisions should align with profitability goals and target market needs to maximize revenue, gain a competitive advantage, and sustain long-term profitability.

### Distribution Channels for Self-Published Entrepreneurs: Exploring Avenues for Product Distribution

Self-publishing has become increasingly popular for entrepreneurs looking to market their own products and reach a wider audience. However, once you have created your product, you need effective distribution channels to make it available to potential customers. In this section, we will explore various avenues for product distribution, both online and offline, including online marketplaces like Amazon and Etsy, physical stores or collaborations with local retailers. We will discuss the advantages and disadvantages of each channel, highlighting their potential impact on profitability.

**Online Marketplaces:**

**a. Amazon:**

**- Advantages:**

i. **Huge customer base:** Amazon has millions of active users, giving your product massive exposure.

ii. **Easy setup:** Setting up a seller account on Amazon is relatively simple, letting entrepreneurs quickly start selling.

iii. **Fulfillment by Amazon (FBA):** FBA enables entrepreneurs to store their products in Amazon's warehouses, providing easy and efficient order fulfillment.

- Disadvantages:

i. **High competition:** With millions of sellers on Amazon, competition for visibility and sales can be intense.

ii. **Amazon fees:** Amazon charges various fees, including referral and fulfillment fees, affecting profit margins.

iii. **Loss of control:** Selling through Amazon means adhering to their policies and rules, leaving entrepreneurs with limited control over customer experience.


b. Etsy:

- Advantages:

i. **Targeted audience:** Etsy specializes in artisanal and handmade products, attracting a unique customer base looking for distinctive items.

ii. **Creative freedom:** Etsy allows entrepreneurs to showcase their creativity and connect with a community of like-minded individuals.

iii. **Lower fees:** Etsy has relatively lower selling fees compared to Amazon, reducing the impact on profitability.

- Disadvantages:

i. **Limited product range:** Etsy is predominantly known for crafts and handmade items, limiting the market potential for certain products.

ii. **Building a brand:** Etsy is a platform where individual sellers thrive, making it challenging for entrepreneurs to build a distinct brand identity.

iii. **Limited visibility outside of Etsy:** Compared to Amazon, Etsy has a narrower reach, potentially limiting exposure to a broader audience.

## 2. Offline Channels:

### a. Physical Stores:

**- Advantages:**

i. **real experience:** Physical stores let customers interact with products physically, enhancing their buying experience.

ii. **Local support:** Collaborations with local retailers can help entrepreneurs build a loyal customer base within their community.

iii. **Personalized selling:** Entrepreneurs can provide personalized customer service, understand buyer preferences, and tailor offerings.

**- Disadvantages:**

i. **Limited reach:** Physical stores have a geographically restricted customer base, affecting the potential for sales growth.

ii. **High overhead costs:** Rent, utilities, and staffing can significantly affect profitability, especially for entrepreneurs with limited resources.

iii. **Need for inventory management:** Maintaining stock levels and managing supply chains can challenge, leading to potential stockouts or excess inventory.

### b. Collaboration with Local Retailers:

**- Advantages:**

i. **Expanded reach:** Collaborating with established retailers lets entrepreneurs access a wider customer base, potentially increasing sales.

ii. **Reduced overhead costs:** Collaborative agreements often involve sharing costs, reducing the financial risk.

**Leveraging Digital Platforms for Monetization:**

Leveraging digital platforms for monetization has become increasingly popular among self-published entrepreneurs. With the right strategies and understanding of their target audience, individuals can effectively monetize their content or knowledge online. There are several effective avenues for making money through digital platforms, including creating and selling online courses, offering consulting services, or engaging in affiliate marketing.

One of the most profitable ways to monetize content or knowledge is by creating and selling online courses. Online learning platforms such as Udemy, Teachable, or Coursera offer an excellent opportunity for entrepreneurs to showcase their knowledge and share it with a global audience. By carefully selecting a niche that aligns with their knowledge and using engaging teaching methods, entrepreneurs can attract learners willing to pay for quality content. Additionally, entrepreneurs can offer supplementary resources or personalized support to enhance the learning experience and increase the value of their courses.

Another way to monetize digital content is by offering consulting services. Many individuals will pay for expert advice or guidance in areas such as business, marketing, finance, health, or personal development. Entrepreneurs can leverage platforms like LinkedIn, Upwork, or their own websites to advertise and offer their consulting services. It is crucial to clearly define the target audience and create service packages that meet their specific needs. By continuously promoting their knowledge and delivering high-quality consultations, entrepreneurs can establish themselves as trusted professionals and attract a loyal clientele.

Affiliate marketing is another popular avenue for monetization, letting entrepreneurs earn a commission by promoting products or services through their digital platforms. By joining affiliate programs of relevant companies or networks like Amazon Associates or ClickBank, entrepreneurs can recommend products that align with their audience's interests. It is essential to maintain transparency and only endorse products that are genuinely valuable to the target audience. By building trust through quality content and honest recommendations, entrepreneurs can generate passive income through affiliate marketing.

Understanding target audience demographics, preferences, and behavior is fundamental when choosing monetization strategies. Entrepreneurs should conduct thorough market research to identify their audience's needs and preferences, ultimately tailoring their offerings to meet those demands effectively. Demographic factors such as age, gender, location, and income can significantly affect the success of monetization strategies. Additionally, entrepreneurs should pay attention to the digital platforms their audience uses and adapt their content or marketing efforts.

Self-published entrepreneurs have many opportunities to monetize their content or knowledge through various digital platforms. Creating and selling online courses, offering consulting services, or engaging in affiliate marketing are a few effective ways to generate income. However, understanding the target audience's demographics and preferences is crucial for selecting the right monetization strategies and maximizing success. By continuously adapting and refining their approach based on audience feedback and market trends, entrepreneurs can unlock the full potential of digital platforms for monetization.

**Collaborative Partnerships for Growth:**

Collaborative partnerships for growth are essential for self-published entrepreneurs looking to expand their businesses and achieve sustainable success. By forming partnerships and collaborations with fellow entrepreneurs in the same industry, numerous advantages can be leveraged to reach mutual growth. Joint marketing efforts, cross-promotion, and shared resources can enhance visibility, expand customer reach, and ultimately increase profitability for both parties involved.

One of the primary advantages of forming partnerships with other self-published entrepreneurs is the opportunity for joint marketing efforts. By pooling resources and sharing marketing costs, entrepreneurs can engage in more extensive and impactful marketing campaigns that would otherwise be unaffordable individually. This enables them to reach a larger target market and effectively communicate their products or services to potential customers. Through joint marketing efforts, entrepreneurs can collectively increase brand recognition, credibility, and attract more customers.

Cross-promotion is a powerful strategy that can significantly help self-published entrepreneurs. By partnering with other entrepreneurs who offer complementary products or services, there is an opportunity to tap into each other's customer base. For example, if one entrepreneur specializes in producing unique handmade jewelry and another focuses on designing handcrafted wooden jewelry boxes, a partnership could lead to cross-promotion where each entrepreneur promotes the other's products to their respective customers. This mutual endorsement helps expand customer reach and can result in increased sales for both parties involved.

Shared resources are another advantage that collaborative partnerships provide for growth. Pooling together resources such as knowledge, skills, equipment, or even finances lets entrepreneurs achieve economies of scale and enhance their overall operational efficiency. For example, self-published authors could share editors, proofreaders, or cover designers, resulting in reduced costs and improved quality of their books. By sharing resources, entrepreneurs can access a wider range of capabilities and gain a competitive edge.

Additionally, forming partnerships and collaborations with other self-published entrepreneurs fosters a supportive and collaborative community. Engaging in knowledge sharing, brainstorming, and learning from each other's experiences can be immensely beneficial. When entrepreneurs come together, they can collectively find innovative solutions to common challenges and learn from each other's successes and failures. This collaborative environment encourages growth and continuous improvement, which ultimately leads to increased profitability.

Collaborative partnerships for growth offer many advantages for self-published entrepreneurs. Joint marketing efforts, cross-promotion, and shared resources can significantly enhance visibility, expand customer reach, and increase profitability for all parties involved. By forming partnerships with like-minded individuals in the self-publishing industry, entrepreneurs can leverage combined strengths, benefit from a wider audience, and foster a supportive community of growth-oriented individuals. Through collaborative partnerships, self-published entrepreneurs can achieve sustainable success in an increasingly competitive market.

## Networking Opportunities Within the Self-Publishing Community:

Networking opportunities within the self-publishing community are crucial for aspiring authors and entrepreneurs looking to enter the industry. Building relationships within this community can open doors to valuable connections, collaborative partnerships, and even potential business opportunities. Attending conferences, joining online forums or groups, and participating in workshops or mastermind groups are all effective ways to network with like-minded individuals, share experiences and insights, and find potential business opportunities.

One of the most traditional networking opportunities within the self-publishing community is attending conferences. These events bring together industry experts, self-published authors, service providers, and other professionals. Conferences provide an environment where individuals can connect, exchange ideas, and build relationships. Attending workshops and panels lets participants learn industry best practices, gain insights from successful authors, and develop valuable insights about various parts of publishing.

In addition to conferences, joining online forums or groups dedicated to self-publishing is another effective networking avenue. Online communities offer a platform to engage in discussions, share experiences, and seek advice from experienced authors and industry professionals. Active participation in these forums can help individuals gain visibility, establish credibility, and forge valuable connections. By sharing knowledge and insights, authors can expand their network and potentially find collaborators, beta readers, editors, or cover designers.

Participating in workshops or mastermind groups is yet another way to network within the self-publishing community. Workshops often focus on specific areas of self-publishing such as marketing, book cover design, or writing techniques. Engaging in these activities exposes authors to industry experts, allowing for meaningful interactions and a chance to learn from those with a wealth of knowledge and experience. Mastermind groups consist of small groups of like-minded individuals who meet regularly to share goals, challenges, and successes. Joining such a group fosters a sense of community and collaboration, providing authors with moral support and access to different perspectives on self-publishing.

The benefits of networking within the self-publishing community are plentiful. Beyond forming meaningful connections, networking can lead to potential business opportunities such as joint venture partnerships or collaborations on book projects. These connections can also result in recommendations for professional services like editors, formatters, or cover designers. Networking provides authors with a support system of individuals who understand the unique challenges and joys of self-publishing.

Networking within the self-publishing community is imperative for authors and entrepreneurs looking to succeed in this industry. Attending conferences, joining online forums or groups, and participating in workshops or mastermind groups offer opportunities to connect with like-minded individuals, share experiences and insights, and find potential business opportunities. By engaging in these networking avenues, authors can expand their network, gain industry knowledge, and build relationships that can contribute to their success as self-published authors.

**Using Social Media for Collaboration and Networking:**

Social media has transformed the way we interact, cooperate, and build relationships in the digital era.. For self-published entrepreneurs, these platforms offer an incredible opportunity to build connections with peers, influencers, and potential customers. In this section, we will discuss the power of social media in fostering collaboration and networking for self-published entrepreneurs. We will also explore effective strategies for using platforms like LinkedIn, Twitter, and Instagram to build a robust network, establish credibility, and leverage collaborations for mutual benefit.

**Building a Network:**

Social media platforms provide an extensive network of professionals, influencers, and like-minded individuals. LinkedIn, known as the professional platform, lets self-published entrepreneurs connect with peers, potential customers, and even industry experts. Building a strong network on LinkedIn involves engaging with relevant content, joining industry groups or communities, and contacting individuals with personalized messages that showcase common interests or knowledge.

Similarly, Twitter's fast-paced and open nature is ideal for connecting with influencers and like-minded professionals. Through following and engaging with relevant accounts, retweeting and sharing valuable content, and participating in relevant Twitter chats or discussions, self-published entrepreneurs can attract followers and foster meaningful connections.

**Establishing Credibility:**

Social media platforms provide an opportunity to establish credibility and showcase knowledge. LinkedIn offers features like endorsements and recommendations, which can be leveraged to highlight skills and experiences. By sharing insightful content, writing thought-provoking articles through LinkedIn's publishing platform, and participating in industry-specific conversations, self-published entrepreneurs can establish themselves as experts in their field.

Twitter, known for its real-time updates, is perfect for showing industry knowledge and thought leadership. Self-published entrepreneurs can engage in conversations with relevant hashtags, share valuable insights, and even participate in industry-specific Twitter chats or conferences. This active participation helps in establishing credibility and attracting potential customers and collaborators.

**Leveraging Collaborations for Mutual Benefit:**

Social media platforms provide a space for entrepreneurs to collaborate with peers and influencers for mutual growth and benefit. Instagram, being a visual platform, lets self-published entrepreneurs collaborate with influencers for sponsored posts, giveaways, or joint product launches. By strategically partnering with influencers who resonate with their target audience, entrepreneurs can tap into a wider customer base and gain exposure.

LinkedIn also offers opportunities for collaborations through shared connections and industry-specific communities. Self-published entrepreneurs can engage in discussions, contribute valuable insights, and actively seek collaborations with professionals possessing complementary skills or knowledge. Collaborative projects, such as co-authoring articles or hosting joint webinars, can help expand reach, attract customers, and establish credibility through association with trusted professionals in the field.

Social media platforms offer tremendous power and potential for self-published entrepreneurs to connect, collaborate, and network. Using LinkedIn, Twitter, and Instagram effectively, entrepreneurs can build a strong network, establish credibility through thought leadership, and leverage collaborations for mutual growth and benefit. The key lies in active engagement, sharing valuable content, and strategic partnerships, ultimately leading to increased visibility, brand recognition, and business opportunities.

**Effective Negotiation and Collaboration Tactics:**

Effective negotiation and collaboration tactics can play a significant role in maximizing profitability for self-published entrepreneurs. By using strategies such as win-win negotiations, building trust, clear communication, and defining clear goals and expectations in collaborative projects, entrepreneurs can ensure successful business outcomes.

Here is guidance on negotiation techniques and effective collaboration practices tailored to self-published entrepreneurs:

## Win-Win Negotiations:

To achieve mutually beneficial outcomes for all parties involved, embrace win-win negotiations. Instead of focusing only on individual interests, explore how both parties can achieve their desired outcomes. Seek solutions that satisfy both your needs and your collaborator's needs to foster long-term partnerships. Remember, a win-lose arrangement can damage relationships and limit future opportunities.

## Building Trust:

Trust is crucial for successful collaborations. Establish trust by showing reliability, accountability, and transparency. Be honest and reliable in all your dealings, meeting deadlines, and fulfilling commitments. Share information openly and avoid keeping crucial details hidden. Trust can be built over time through consistent behavior and open communication channels.

## Clear Communication:

Open and effective communication is essential for smooth collaborations. Express your ideas, expectations, and concerns while listening to your collaborators. Use both verbal and written communication to ensure clarity. Summarize agreements reached and share them in writing to avoid misunderstandings. Encourage regular updates, feedback, and ask for clarifications whenever needed.

## Defining Clear Goals and Expectations:

Defining goals and expectations is crucial for a successful collaboration. Set specific, measurable, attainable, relevant, and time-bound (SMART) goals. Collaboratively establish project milestones, responsibilities, and deadlines. Establish a shared understanding of expectations, such as the quality of work, timeliness, and deliverables. Defining these parts reduces confusion and helps maintain focus and accountability.

## Establishing a Legal Agreement:

Before beginning any collaborative project, establish a legal agreement to protect both parties' interests. Outline the project scope, financial arrangements, intellectual property rights, confidentiality, and dispute resolution methods. Engage legal professionals to draft the agreement to ensure it covers all necessary parts and safeguards your interests.

**Assessing Collaborator Fit:**

Choosing the right collaborators is critical to successful outcomes. Evaluate potential partners based on their expertise, track record, and shared values. Consider their commitment to excellence, willingness to communicate openly, and ability to resolve conflicts constructively. A compatible collaborator can bring complementary skills and resources, enhancing profitability.

**Nurturing Long-Term Relationships:**

Maximize profitability by nurturing long-term relationships with collaborators. Maintain open lines of communication, show appreciation for their contributions, and regularly provide updates on shared projects or potential new ventures. Foster a collaborative culture of ongoing improvement, sharing knowledge, and supporting each other's growth. Such relationships can lead to repeat collaborations and referrals, ultimately boosting profitability.

Effective negotiation and collaboration tactics are essential for self-published entrepreneurs to maximize profitability. Embrace win-win negotiations, build trust, maintain clear communication, establish clear goals and expectations, create legal agreements, when necessary, assess collaborator fit, and nurture long-term relationships. By following these strategies, entrepreneurs can ensure successful collaborations, enhance profitability, and unlock new opportunities in the self-publishing industry.

**Chapter Summary:**

The chapter discusses the importance of strategic pricing aligned with profitability goals and target audience needs. It examines pricing approaches like cost-plus, value-based, and dynamic pricing.

Distribution channels are explored including online marketplaces like Amazon and Etsy which offer exposure but can limit control, and physical stores which have higher overhead costs but allow customer interactions.

Monetization through online courses, consulting services, and affiliate marketing leverages digital platforms.

Collaborative partnerships for growth via joint marketing, cross-promotion, and shared resources are highlighted to expand reach.

Networking opportunities within the self-publishing community exist at conferences, online forums, workshops, and mastermind groups.

Social media enables connections with peers, influencers, and customers to build credibility and foster collaborations.

Effective negotiation tactics involve win-win solutions, clear communication, defined expectations, and nurturing long-term relationships.

The chapter provides guidance on optimizing pricing, choosing distribution channels, generating online income, collaborating for growth, networking, and negotiating to maximize profitability.

**In our next chapter…**

In this illuminating chapter, we delve deep into the essential strategies for maximizing success in the self-publishing world.

We explore the undeniable power of building authentic relationships with your readers, leveraging the capabilities of social media and email marketing to foster these connections.

Recognizing the importance of direct engagement, the chapter provides insight on hosting in-person events and book signings to interact closely with your readers.

We underline the importance of feedback and reviews, not only as a tool for improvement but also as a direct link to express gratitude and appreciation toward your audience.

The chapter also delves into the realm of strategic pricing, distributions, and monetization, providing guidance on how to optimize these parts for profitability.

The potential of networking and collaborations, both online and offline, is outlined, with a focus on the significant role these strategies play in expanding your reach.

As a highlight, we discuss the art of negotiation, emphasizing the importance of clear communication and long-term relationships.

This chapter is a comprehensive guide for anyone looking to strengthen their self-publishing journey, providing valuable insights and strategies to nurture relationships, maximize profitability, and ultimately, achieve success.

∼

## CHAPTER FIFTEEN

# BUILDING A SUSTAINABLE AUTHOR BUSINESS BEYOND THE FIRST BOOK

THE BENEFITS **of a Sustainable Author Business:**

**Increased income potential:** A sustainable author business lets authors build multiple streams of income through books, speaking engagements, merchandise, and other creative avenues, thus maximizing their earning potential.

**Wider audience reach:** By adopting sustainable practices, authors can leverage various marketing and distribution channels to expand their reach beyond traditional publishing platforms. This enables them to connect with readers worldwide and tap into new markets and demographics.

**Establishing a loyal fan base:** Building a sustainable author business fosters strong connections with readers, enabling authors to cultivate a dedicated fan base. These loyal readers often become brand advocates, spreading positive word-of-mouth, and bolstering an author's reputation and sales.

**Opportunities for creative collaboration:** Sustainable author businesses offer authors many opportunities for collaboration with other authors, illustrators, filmmakers, and other creative professionals. This not only enhances their creative output but also introduces them to new audiences and markets.

**Adaptability and longevity:** Sustainable author businesses focus on long-term success by embracing continuous learning, adaptability, and innovation. This enables authors to navigate changing market trends, technology advancements, and evolving reader preferences, ensuring the longevity of their careers.

**Freedom and flexibility:** By building a sustainable author business, authors can enjoy greater freedom and flexibility in their work. They have the autonomy to choose their projects, set their own schedules, and pursue their creative passions while still earning a steady income.

**Legacy and impact:** A sustainable author business enables authors to leave a legacy and make a meaningful impact on their readers and communities. By building a strong brand and creating timeless stories, authors can impart knowledge, inspire others, and shape cultural conversations for generations to come.

### Understanding The Role of Branding and Positioning:

### Introduction to Branding and Positioning:

In today's highly saturated literary landscape, leveraging branding and positioning has become imperative for authors to stand out and succeed. These two interconnected elements play a crucial role in distinguishing and promoting a writer's work, letting them stand out from the crowd and capture the attention of their target audience.

Branding is establishing a distinct name, identity, and reputation for a product or service. It goes beyond a simple logo or tagline, encompassing the overall perception and image associated with a particular author or their body of work. Successful branding helps to create a recognizable and memorable impression among readers, making it easier for them to identify and choose a specific author's books amidst a sea of alternatives.

Positioning, on the other hand, deals with how an author's work is positioned or perceived relative to their competitors. It involves identifying and occupying a distinct and useful place in the minds of readers, setting oneself apart from others in the industry. Effective positioning is crucial as it influences consumer perceptions, preferences, and ultimately, purchasing decisions.

The importance of branding and positioning cannot be overstated in the literature market. With many talented authors vying for readers' attention, a strong and well-defined brand can serve as a powerful differentiator, helping authors establish a loyal and dedicated readership. Through a compelling brand, authors can communicate their unique voice, style, and values, thus fostering a sense of trust and familiarity with their target audience.

Additionally, effective positioning enables authors to efficiently target their desired readership and tailor their marketing efforts. By understanding their target audience's preferences, needs, and desires, authors can position their work in a way that aligns with readers' expectations, increasing the likelihood of attracting their attention and cultivating a loyal fan base.

Branding and positioning can play a significant role in an author's long-term success and sustainability. A strong brand not only helps with initial book sales but also enhances an author's credibility and authority in the industry. A well-positioned author will be better equipped to navigate and adapt to the evolving literary landscape, ensuring their relevance and continued success.

Branding and positioning are pivotal ideas in the competitive market of literature. Through effective branding, authors can establish a recognizable and distinctive identity for their work, while positioning lets them occupy a unique and useful space in readers' minds. By harnessing these ideas, authors can differentiate themselves from their peers, connect with their target audience, and ultimately thrive in the ever-evolving landscape of literature.

**Impact Of Branding on Author Identity:**

The impact of branding on the author's identity cannot be understated. In today's crowded literary market, authors face fierce competition to capture readers' attention and establish a distinct identity. However, through strategic branding efforts, authors can effectively differentiate themselves, build a loyal following, and leave a lasting impression on their readers. This chapter aims to explore how branding influences an author's identity and the ways in which it can help them succeed in the publishing industry.

**Building a Unique Identity:**

Branding plays a crucial role in helping authors create a unique identity that sets them apart from their peers. By carefully crafting their brand image, authors can communicate their distinctive style, genre, and overall message to their target audience. This includes elements such as author logos, taglines, and consistent visual and verbal cues that help readers recognize and connect with their work. Through effective branding, authors can solidify their identity in readers' minds, making them easily identifiable and memorable.

**Standing Out:**

In a saturated literary market, authors must stand out from the competition. Strategic branding efforts can provide authors with the tools to differentiate themselves and capture readers' attention. By understanding their target audience and aligning their brand with readers' preferences, authors can tailor their marketing strategies and book presentations. This may involve using innovative promotional tactics, using social media platforms, or collaborating with influencers in the literary community. With an effective branding strategy, authors can effectively rise above the noise and establish a distinctive presence.

**Developing a Loyal Following:**

Branding plays a significant role in building a loyal fan base for authors. A strong brand identity fosters an emotional connection between authors and their readers, creating a sense of loyalty and trust. By consistently delivering high-quality content and embodying the values associated with their brand, authors can cultivate a devoted following that eagerly expects their new releases. Such a loyal audience not only helps authors achieve success with their current work but also serves as a foundation for future endeavors, enabling them to expand their reach and influence.

## Leaving a Lasting Impression:

Branding is not only about capturing readers' attention but also about leaving a lasting impression in their minds. A well-defined brand identity lets authors develop a reputation for reliability, credibility, and consistency. By consistently delivering on their promises and meeting readers' expectations, authors can build trust and loyalty, resulting in a lasting impact on their audience. This positive author-reader relationship encourages word-of-mouth promotion and generates a ripple effect, attracting new readers and expanding the author's reach.

Regarding author identity, strategic branding plays a pivotal role in differentiating authors from their peers and helping them succeed in the competitive publishing industry. By carefully crafting their brand image, authors can build a unique identity that resonates with readers, ultimately leading to increased recognition, a loyal following, and a lasting impact. Embracing the power of branding lets authors stand out, make their mark, and prove themselves to be significant figures in the literary world.

## Differentiation Through Branding:

In today's saturated market, authors face an uphill battle in getting their books noticed by readers. With countless authors vying for attention, it has become imperative to differentiate oneself from the crowd. This section will delve into various branding techniques that authors can employ to stand out and capture readers' interests. It emphasizes the significance of discovering a unique selling point and effectively conveying it to potential readers.

## Discover Your Unique Selling Point:

Before crafting a brand, authors must identify what sets them apart from others in their genre. This can be achieved by analyzing their writing style, themes, and personal experiences. Understanding your unique strengths and perspectives will lay the foundation for establishing a strong brand identity.

### Define Your Target Audience:

Authors must determine the ideal readership for their books. By understanding the demographics, interests, and preferences of their target audience, they can tailor their branding efforts. This enables authors to effectively communicate their unique selling point to those most likely to appreciate it.

### Develop Your Brand Identity:

Once the unique selling point and target audience have been identified, authors can create an authentic brand identity that resonates with their readers. This involves choosing a brand name, logo, color scheme, and overall visual aesthetic that reflects the author's personality and writing style. Consistency across all branding materials will help establish a recognizable and enduring brand identity.

### Craft a Compelling Author Bio:

An engaging author biography plays a pivotal role in differentiating an author. By highlighting personal experiences, interests, achievements, or writing processes that mirror their unique selling point, authors can show a genuine connection with readers. A well-crafted bio enhances readers' understanding of the author's background and motivations, fostering a sense of trust and loyalty.

### Leverage Social Media:

Social media provides authors with an influential means to cultivate their brand and engage with readers in the digital era. By maintaining an active and consistent presence on platforms relevant to their target audience, authors can share insights, updates, and engaging content that reinforces their unique selling point. Authentically engaging with readers through comments and conversations helps establish a loyal following.

### Collaborate and Network:

Authors can further differentiate themselves by collaborating with other authors, influencers, or professionals in related fields. Joint projects, co-authorship, or guest appearances can expose their unique brand to new audiences and create valuable connections. Collaborations can also enhance an author's credibility and reinforce their unique selling point.

**Establish Author Expertise:**

To solidify their unique selling point, authors can establish themselves as experts or thought leaders in their field. This can be achieved by writing articles, guest posts, or giving talks related to their genre or niche. Offering valuable insights and expertise not only helps differentiate an author but also fosters trust and credibility among readers.

**Engage with Readers:**

Last, authors must consistently interact with their readers. Responding to reviews, organizing reader events, or hosting online discussions through blogs or social media platforms enables authors to connect directly with their audience. This personal touch reinforces their unique selling point and helps create a loyal readership base.

Differentiation through branding is vital for authors looking to rise above the competition. By identifying a unique selling point, understanding the target audience, and effectively communicating their brand identity, authors can differentiate themselves from the multitude of authors. Using branding techniques, such as crafting a compelling author bio, leveraging social media, collaborating, establishing knowledge, and engaging with readers, will help authors establish a strong and lasting brand presence in the literary world.

**Positioning Strategies for Authors:**

Positioning is a vital part for authors who aim to establish a strong presence in their target market. By strategically positioning themselves, authors can effectively reach their intended audience, differentiate themselves in a competitive genre, and leverage their personal knowledge or experiences to gain a competitive advantage. This chapter will delve into various positioning strategies that authors can employ to achieve success.

**Identifying the Right Audience:**

The first step toward effective positioning is identifying the target audience for your book. Understanding the demographics, interests, and preferences of your ideal readers will help you tailor your marketing efforts and resonate with them on a deeper level. Conducting market research, using online tools to analyze reader profiles, and seeking feedback from early readers can aid in identifying the right audience for your work.

**Differentiating in a Crowded Genre:**

In a saturated book market, standing out from competitors is crucial. Authors can differentiate themselves by focusing on unique parts of their book, such as distinctive writing style, unusual plot twists, or unconventional characters. Researching the existing books in the same genre and analyzing their strengths and weaknesses can provide insights into how to position your work differently. Crafting a compelling author brand that resonates with readers can also help in distinguishing yourself from others.

**Leveraging Personal Expertise or Experiences:**

Authors who have personal knowledge or have had unique experiences can use them as positioning strategies. By infusing their knowledge into their writing and positioning themselves as subject matter experts, authors can attract readers interested in that field. Sharing personal experiences or inspiring stories through social media, interviews, or blog posts can further enhance this positioning strategy.

**Creating a Strong Online Presence:**

Authors today have a tremendous advantage in reaching their target audience through various online platforms. Building a strong online presence by having an author website, active social media accounts, and engaging with readers through blogs or newsletters can position authors as accessible and approachable. Consistently presenting valuable content, sharing behind-the-scenes insights, and engaging with the audience can foster a loyal following.

## Collaborating and Networking:

Collaborating with other authors or influencers within the industry can be a compelling positioning strategy. Joint author events, co-writing projects, or cross-promotions can help expand your reach and tap into new audiences. Networking with literary agents, publishers, book reviewers, and bloggers can also provide opportunities to enhance your positioning through endorsements, reviews, or interviews.

Positioning strategies play a crucial role in determining an author's success. By identifying the right audience, differentiating from competitors, leveraging personal knowledge, creating a strong online presence, and collaborating with others, authors can effectively position themselves within their target market. Using these strategies along with consistent effort and quality content can maximize an author's chances of success and establish a strong presence within the crowded literary landscape.

## The Power of Personal Branding:

The power of personal branding cannot be underestimated in the world of authors and writers. It is more than a logo or a catchy tagline; it is the embodiment of your unique personality, values, and beliefs. In a crowded marketplace, where countless authors are vying for attention, a strong personal brand can set you apart and help you establish a loyal following of readers.

Personal branding is about authentically expressing who you are as an individual and as an author. It is about bringing your true self to the table and letting readers connect with you on a deeper level. When readers resonate with your personal brand, they are more likely to become invested in your work and support you throughout your writing journey.

One strategy to create a strong personal brand is through authentic storytelling. Share your personal experiences, struggles, and triumphs in a way that resonates with your target audience. By being vulnerable and genuine, you invite readers to connect with you on an emotional level. This not only deepens the bond between you and your readers, but it also helps you stand out in a sea of generic authors.

Another important part of personal branding is fostering a connection with your readers. Engage with them on social media, respond to their comments and messages, and create opportunities for dialogue. Show genuine interest in their lives and opinions. By doing so, you create a community around your personal brand, where readers feel valued, heard, and engaged. This can lead to increased loyalty and word-of-mouth promotion, as readers become your biggest advocates.

Consistency is key regarding personal branding. Make sure your brand message and values are reflected in everything you do, from your writing style to your social media content. This cohesiveness builds trust and familiarity with your audience, making it easier for them to identify and connect with your personal brand.

Personal branding is not about creating a false persona or catering to popular trends. It is about showcasing the authentic, unique qualities that make you who you are. Embrace your individuality, and let your personal brand reflect your true self. When readers see your authenticity shine through, they are more likely to develop a genuine connection and become loyal fans.

Personal branding is a powerful tool for authors. By leveraging your own personality, values, and beliefs, you can establish a strong author identity that resonates with readers. Through strategies such as authentic storytelling and fostering a connection with your audience, you can build a loyal following and stand out in a crowded marketplace. Remember, your personal brand is your secret weapon – use it wisely and watch your writing career soar.

**Using Social Media For Branding:**

In today's hyper-connected world, social media has become an indispensable tool for authors to effectively establish and communicate their brand. Platforms like Twitter, Instagram, and LinkedIn offer unique opportunities for authors to visually showcase their brand and engage with readers on a personal level. This section will delve into the role of social media in author branding and explore various strategies to leverage its potential.

### Establishing a Consistent Brand Identity:

To effectively use social media for branding, authors must first establish a consistent brand identity. This includes determining core values, defining the target audience, and crafting a unique brand voice. By aligning these elements, authors can resonate with readers and create a recognizable brand presence across various social media platforms.

### Choosing the Right Platforms:

Different social media platforms cater to different audiences and provide distinct engagement opportunities. Authors should carefully choose platforms that best align with their brand and target audience. Twitter, with its fast-paced nature, is ideal for engaging in real-time conversations and promoting new releases. Instagram's visual nature allows authors to showcase their books, writing process, and personal life, creating a more intimate connection with readers. LinkedIn presents a professional platform to emphasize industry knowledge and connect with fellow authors and industry professionals.

### Visual Communication and Branding:

Successful author branding on social media relies heavily on visual elements. By curating appealing visuals, authors can effectively capture readers' attention and communicate their brand identity. Eye-catching book covers, aesthetically pleasing quotes, and behind-the-scenes glimpses of the writing process are popular ways authors can visually engage with readers and reinforce their brand.

### Engaging with Readers:

Social media offers authors a unique opportunity to directly engage with their readers in real-time. By responding to comments, starting conversations, and participating in discussions, authors can establish a personal connection with their audience. This engagement not only strengthens the relationship between the author and readers but also builds a loyal following, generating organic promotion and word-of-mouth recommendations.

**Leveraging Social Media Features:**

Social media platforms constantly introduce new features and updates to enhance user experience. Authors should stay updated with these developments and leverage them to amplify their brand presence. From using Twitter's trending hashtags to host live Q&A sessions to using Instagram Stories for interactive book quizzes, authors can creatively leverage the latest social media features to further establish their brand and engage with readers.

Using the power of social media for author branding is crucial in today's competitive publishing landscape. By effectively using platforms like Twitter, Instagram, and LinkedIn, authors can visually communicate their brand, engage with readers, and strengthen their overall positioning. This chapter has provided valuable insights and strategies for authors to harness the potential of social media, ultimately widening their reach and building a strong author brand.

**Building A Brand Strategy:**

Building a strong brand is essential for businesses to differentiate themselves from competitors and connect with their target audience. A comprehensive brand strategy helps establish a clear identity and creates an emotional connection with customers. This final section provides step-by-step instructions on creating a brand strategy that encompasses defining brand elements, establishing a brand voice, implementing consistent branding across platforms, and tracking and adjusting the brand strategy as needed.

**Defining Brand Elements:**

The first step in building a brand strategy is to define the brand elements. These elements include the brand name, logo, tagline, color palette, typography, and visual imagery. It is crucial to choose brand elements that align with the company's values, personality, and target audience. Conduct thorough research and collaborate with designers to create brand elements that are memorable, distinctive, and visually appealing.

### Creating a Brand Voice:

A brand voice represents the personality and tone of the brand's communication. It determines the language, style, and messaging used across all platforms. To create a brand voice, consider the brand's core values, target audience, and competitive landscape. Create guidelines for the language and tone of communication, ensuring consistency across various touchpoints. Use the brand voice to evoke emotions, convey key messages, and engage with the target audience authentically.

### Implementing Consistent Branding Across Platforms:

Consistency is the key to building a strong brand. It is essential to implement consistent branding across all platforms, including websites, social media, packaging, advertisements, and customer interactions. Make sure the brand elements, including the logo, color palette, typography, and imagery, are consistently used across all touchpoints. This consistency helps customers recognize and remember the brand, building trust and loyalty.

### Tracking and Adjusting the Brand Strategy:

Building a brand strategy is an ongoing process. It is crucial to track the effectiveness of the brand strategy and make changes as needed. Regularly evaluate key metrics such as brand awareness, customer perception, and market positioning. Conduct market research and analyze customer feedback to identify areas for improvement. Adjust the brand strategy making necessary updates to brand elements, messaging, or communication channels to stay relevant and resonate with the target audience.

Building a brand strategy is a multi-step process that requires careful consideration and continuous evaluation. By defining brand elements, establishing a brand voice, implementing consistent branding across platforms, and tracking and adjusting the strategy, businesses can create a strong brand that resonates with their target audience. Remember, consistency and authenticity are key to building brand loyalty and establishing a distinct identity in today's competitive market.

**Building An Author Platform for Long-Term Success:**

**Introduction to Building an Author Platform:**

Establishing an author platform is a crucial element for attaining lasting success as a writer in the current digital landscape. Gone are the days when writers could rely solely on the quality of their books to attract readers. With the exponential growth of technology and the rise of social media, authors must now establish a strong online presence to effectively connect with their audience and establish themselves as notable figures in the industry.

An author platform refers to the methods and tools an author uses to showcase their work, engage with their readers, and build a loyal following. It includes various online platforms such as websites, blogs, social media profiles, and email newsletters. Effectively using these platforms is crucial for authors who aspire to gain visibility, attract publishers, sell books, and establish a sustainable writing career.

One of the primary reasons to focus on building an author platform is to establish credibility and authority in the literary world. By consistently providing valuable content and engaging with readers on various platforms, authors can position themselves as experts in their niche or genre. This can significantly influence readers' purchasing decisions and strengthen their trust in the author's work, ultimately leading to increased book sales and a broader fan base.

Additionally, an author platform enables writers to connect directly with their target audience. Through social media channels like Twitter,

Instagram, and Facebook, authors can engage in conversations with readers, answer their questions, and gain insights into their preferences. By cultivating this direct line of communication, authors can better understand their audience's needs and tailor their writing and marketing strategies.

Having a robust author platform provides writers with opportunities for collaboration, networking, and partnerships. Authors can participate in guest blogging, podcasts, interviews, and other promotional activities to expand their reach and establish connections with fellow authors, influencers, and industry professionals. Collaborative efforts can amplify an author's visibility and introduce their work to new audiences, ultimately fostering long-term success.

Last, an author platform helps in building a loyal and dedicated fan base. By consistently providing engaging content and staying connected through newsletters or blog subscriptions, authors can cultivate a community of readers who eagerly anticipate their next release. This dedicated fan base not only supports and promotes the author's work but also becomes an asset when generating buzz, positive reviews, and word-of-mouth recommendations.

Creating an author platform has become indispensable for writers looking to achieve enduring success in the digital literary landscape of today. With the power of technology and social media, authors can establish credibility, connect with their target audience, collaborate with industry professionals, and build a loyal fan base. Embracing these platforms and consistently investing time and effort in them can lead to increased book sales, wider recognition, and a thriving writing career.

### The Role of a Website: A Central Hub for Author, Books, and Content

A thoughtfully designed website is an essential asset for authors to build connections with readers, exhibit their writing, and interact with their audience in the digital era. It acts as a central hub where readers can learn about the author, discover their books, and explore their content. Let's delve into the different aspects of how a website plays a significant role in author-reader interaction and promotion.

First, a website provides valuable information about the author. Readers often want to know more about the person behind the books they love. A well-structured "About Me" section on the website lets authors share their biographies, their writing journey, and their inspiration for the stories they create. This adds a personal touch, enabling readers to develop a deeper connection with the author and their literary works.

A website becomes an online catalog, letting readers browse through an author's books. Organizing books by genre or series helps readers explore an author's complete repertoire while getting a sense of the writing style and themes. Detailed summaries, sample chapters, and reviews can further entice readers into buying the books. Including links to reputable online retailers or the author's preferred purchasing platform lets readers conveniently buy the books that capture their interest.

Besides serving as an online bookstore, a website also serves as a platform for engaging with the readers. Incorporating a blog or regularly updated content section enables authors to share exclusive insights, behind-the-scenes details, and news about upcoming releases. By offering a glimpse into their creative process, authors can make readers feel involved in their literary journey. This interactive element elevates the reader experience, fostering a loyal fan base and piquing interest in future releases.

Additionally, a well-designed website becomes a necessary platform for promoting upcoming events such as book signings, speaking engagements, or virtual author Q&A sessions. Readers can easily find information on these events, letting them interact with the author in person or virtually. This personal interaction helps create enduring connections and positive word-of-mouth promotion among readers.

A website can provide a way for readers to contact the author directly. Including a contact form or an email address lets readers send messages, feedback, or inquiries. Authors can respond promptly, making readers feel valued and deepening their connection. This engagement can lead to valuable insights and even inspire future writing endeavors.

A well-designed website plays a pivotal role as a central hub in an author's online presence. It serves as a platform for readers to learn about the author, discover their books, and engage with their content. Through detailed information, captivating book summaries, interactive blog posts, and opportunities for direct communication, a website enhances the reader experience, establishes reader-author connections, and fosters a loyal fan base. In today's competitive literary landscape, a well-crafted website is indispensable in showcasing an author's talent and captivating readers worldwide.

**Harnessing the Power of Social Media: Examining Different Platforms for Authors**

Social media has revolutionized the way authors can connect with their audience, share updates about their work, and foster a sense of community. This chapter aims to discuss various social media platforms and provide strategies for authors to effectively use these tools to engage with their readership.

**Facebook:**

With billions of monthly active users, Facebook offers authors a vast potential audience. Create an author page to share updates on your writing process, book releases, and upcoming events. Engage with your audience by asking questions, running giveaways, or conducting live Q&A sessions. Join relevant groups or start your own book club to foster a community around your work.

**Twitter:**

Twitter's fast-paced nature makes it suitable for concise updates and quick interactions with your audience. Craft compelling tweets with book quotes, writing tips, or behind-the-scenes insights. Participate in relevant conversations using hashtags related to your genre or literary discussions. Retweet and interact with your readers, fellow authors, and book reviewers to build lasting connections.

**Instagram:**

Leverage Instagram's visual appeal to captivate your audience. Share aesthetically pleasing book covers, author photos, or snapshots from your writing process. Use Instagram Stories to provide exclusive sneak peeks and engage your followers by running polls or asking for their opinions. Engage with other authors and bookstagrammers by commenting and liking their posts to expand your reach.

**YouTube:**

For authors comfortable with video content, YouTube provides a powerful avenue to connect with readers. Create an author channel to discuss your books, share book trailers, offer writing advice, or conduct interviews with other authors. Encourage viewers to subscribe and comment, fostering a community around your content.

**Goodreads:**

As a dedicated platform for readers, Goodreads offers authors an excellent opportunity to connect with their audience. Create an author profile and engage in discussions on relevant book forums. Encourage readers to leave ratings and reviews for your work and respond to their feedback. Host giveaways and answer reader questions to build an active and engaged community.

**TikTok:**

This emerging platform provides authors with a unique way to showcase their creativity. Create short, engaging videos with book recommendations, reading challenges, or snippets from your work. Use popular TikTok trends to attract a wider audience and collaborate with other authors or booktubers for cross-promotion.

Social media platforms provide authors an invaluable opportunity to connect with their audience, share updates about their work, and foster an engaged community. Using platforms like Facebook, Twitter, Instagram, YouTube, Goodreads, and TikTok, authors can effectively promote their books, build lasting relationships, and continuously engage with their readers. With the right strategy, authors can harness the power of social media to amplify their reach, influence, and impact as writers.

## The Significance of An Email List:

The significance of an email list for authors cannot be overstated in today's digital age. Building a strong and engaged email list lets authors directly connect with their readers, share exclusive content, and effectively promote new releases. In this section, we will delve into why an email list is essential for authors and provide valuable tips on how to grow and maintain it.

### Direct and Personal Communication:

One of the most significant advantages of an email list is the ability to communicate directly with your readers. Unlike social media platforms where algorithms determine who sees your content, email makes sure your message reaches the intended recipients. By having an email list, you can create a personal connection with your readers, fostering a sense of loyalty and trust.

### Sharing Exclusive Content:

An email list provides an excellent opportunity to share exclusive content with your subscribers. This could range from early access to upcoming book chapters or sneak peeks at cover reveals. By offering exclusive content to your email subscribers, you make them feel special and appreciated. This strengthens the bond between you and your readers.

**Effective Book Promotion:**

When promoting new releases, an email list is an invaluable asset. Your subscribers have shown interest in your work by opting to receive updates from you. This makes them more likely to be receptive to your book promotions. By sending out targeted emails about your new releases, you can generate excitement, increase pre-orders, and boost sales.

Now that we understand the significance of an email list for authors, let's explore tips on how to grow and maintain it effectively:

**Engage With Your Readers:**

Engagement is key to growing and maintaining an email list. Encourage readers to sign up by offering incentives such as a free short story or a discount on your books. Once they subscribe, regularly engage with them through personalized emails, asking for their feed-back or sharing interesting updates about your writing journey.

**Provide Valuable Content:**

To keep your subscribers engaged, it is crucial to provide them with valuable content. This can include book recommendations, writing tips, or behind-the-scenes insights into your creative process. Keeping your emails informative and entertaining will make readers look forward to hearing from you and prevent them from unsubscribing.

**Segment Your E-mail List:**

Segmenting your email list involves dividing your subscribers into smaller groups based on their preferences and interests. This lets you send targeted emails that cater to their specific needs. For example, you can create separate segments for readers interested in different genres or those who prefer audiobooks. By tailoring your messages, you increase the likelihood of engagement and conversions.

**Be Consistent and Respectful:**

Maintain a consistent schedule when sending out emails to your subscribers. Whether it's a monthly newsletter or weekly updates, be reliable and avoid bombarding readers with frequent, irrelevant emails. Additionally, always focus on their privacy by securely storing their information and adhering to data protection regulations.

Building and maintaining an email list is crucial for authors. It enables direct communication with readers, offers a platform to share exclusive content, and is an effective tool for promoting new releases. By engaging with readers, providing valuable content, segmenting your list, and respecting their preferences, you can grow a strong and loyal email community that supports your writing career.

### Creating An Engaging Author Brand: Exploring the Path to Building Trust and Standing Out in The Crowded Marketplace

In today's saturated book market, authors need more than a compelling story to capture readers' attention. Developing a strong personal brand has become crucial for authors to build trust and stand out from the sea of competitors. By maintaining consistent messaging, visual elements, and tone, authors can create an engaging brand that resonates with their target audience and establishes long-lasting relationships.

### Crafting Consistent Messaging:

Authors must identify their unique selling points and core values to create consistent messaging that permeates throughout their brand. Ask yourself, "What makes my writing style, genre, or themes distinct?" Incorporate those distinctive parts into your author bio, website, social media profiles, and book descriptions. By consistently emphasizing your strengths, readers will clearly understand what to expect from your work.

### Visual Elements That Reflect Your Voice:

Visuals play a vital role in creating an engaging author brand. Design a professional author logo or choose a font style that reflects your writing voice. These visual elements should be present on your book covers, website, social media posts, and promotional materials. Consistency is key in visually representing your brand, creating a cohesive and recognizable identity that readers will associate with your work.

**Tone That Connects With Readers:**

The tone authors use in their communication is another crucial aspect of building an engaging brand. This tone should align with the genre and target audience of your books. If your writing is humorous and lighthearted, use a similar tone in your social media interactions, blog posts, and author interviews. The tone should be authentic and reflect your personality, letting readers connect with you on a more personal level.

**Establishing Trust Through Engagement:**

Building trust with readers is essential for long-term success. Engage with your audience by responding to comments, emails, and social media messages promptly and thoughtfully. Be approachable and genuine and try to foster a sense of community through author events, readings, or online discussions. Regularly provide valuable content, such as writing tips, book recommendations, or behind-the-scenes insights, to show your dedication to your readers beyond promoting your own work.

**Leveraging Social Media Platforms:**

In this digital era, social media is the ideal platform to showcase your author brand and connect directly with readers. Choose the platforms where your target audience is most active, whether it's Twitter, Instagram, Facebook, or a combination of them. Share updates about your writing process, excerpts from your work, and engage in conversations relevant to your genre. Through consistent and authentic interactions, you can build a loyal following and strengthen your author's brand.

Creating an engaging author brand requires careful consideration of consistent messaging, visual elements, and tone. By emphasizing what makes your writing unique, using visuals that reflect your voice, and communicating with readers in an engaging and trustworthy manner, you can develop a strong personal brand that resonates and stands out in the crowded marketplace. With time, dedication, and a thoughtful approach, you can build a loyal base of readers who will eagerly await your next book and recommend your work to others.

## Leveraging Collaborations and Partnerships:

In today's interconnected world, building a successful platform or brand as an author, influencer, or organization is a matter of reaching and engaging with the right audience. While individual efforts can yield results, leveraging collaborations and partnerships can provide a powerful boost in meeting these goals. In this section, we will discuss the benefits of collaborating with other authors, influencers, or organizations, highlighting how such partnerships can help reach new audiences, expand one's platform, and create mutually beneficial relationships.

## Expanding Reach and Accessing New Audiences:

One of the primary advantages of collaborations and partnerships is the ability to access new audiences. By teaming up with other authors, influencers, or organizations with a complementary following, you can tap into their established network and introduce your work to a fresh set of eyes. This can help expand your reach far beyond your existing audience and provide an opportunity to connect with individuals who may have never found your content otherwise.

For authors, collaborating with fellow writers can lead to cross-promotion opportunities, book bundles or collections, and joint events such as panel discussions or virtual book tours. By mutually promoting each other's work or organizing joint marketing campaigns, authors can attract readers interested in similar genres or writing styles.

For influencers, partnering with other influential individuals in related niches allows for cross-exposure to each other's audiences. By highlighting each other's content, recommending one another, or even creating joint content, influencers can introduce themselves to new followers who might share interests or passions.

For organizations, collaborations enable access to untapped markets and audience segments. Partnerships could range from co-hosting events, creating joint initiatives, or even working together on marketing and public relations campaigns. Sharing resources and knowledge can help organizations collectively leverage their strengths and present a more comprehensive, attractive offering to potential customers or stakeholders.

**Expanding Platforms and Content Variability:**

Collaborations and partnerships also allow for the expansion of one's own platform or content offerings. By teaming up with others, authors, influencers, or organizations can tap into diverse knowledge, perspectives, and styles, thus enriching their own output and appealing to a broader audience.

For authors, collaborating with fellow writers can create anthologies, co-authored books, or joint projects that combine different writing styles or themes. This not only diversifies the authors' portfolios but also lets them tap into each other's fan base and readership.

For influencers, collaborations may involve hosting guest posts, participating in shared interviews, and even creating joint YouTube videos or podcasts. This variety of content not only keeps followers engaged but also attracts new listeners or viewers interested in the collaborator's knowledge or subject matter.

For organizations, partnerships can help in launching co-branded products or services, combining domain expertise to create innovative offerings, or simply diversifying their content strategies. An organization's collaboration with another can lead to new market opportunities, a fresh approach, or the development of new solutions that cater to a wider range of customer needs.

**Building Mutually Beneficial Relationships:**

Beyond simply expanding reach and diversifying content, collaborations and partnerships have immense potential for building strong, mutually beneficial relationships. By working together, authors, influencers, or organizations can share knowledge, resources, and gain exposure to different perspectives or audiences.

Authors can not only gain inspiration from their collaborators but also benefit from shared marketing resources, support during book launches, or access to different publishing platforms.

Influencers can collaborate with each other to learn and grow, sharing insights, tips, and tricks that have worked well for their respective journeys. Additionally, joining forces can lead to increased brand credibility and exposure to new sponsorship or partnership opportunities.

For organizations, partnering with other like-minded entities can result in sharing best practices, industry expertise, and the potential for knowledge exchange. Such collaborations can reinforce the reputation and trustworthiness of both organizations, expanding their network and helping with future partnerships with new stakeholders.

In the ever-evolving landscape of authors, influencers, and organizations, leveraging collaborations and partnerships is an effective strategy for reaching new audiences, expanding platforms, and building mutually beneficial relationships. By tapping into the power of collaboration, individuals and entities can unlock new opportunities, diversify their content, and establish themselves as influential players in their respective fields. Embracing collaboration not only benefits individual growth but also contributes to the collective progress and development of the entire community.

**Nurturing And Evolving the Author Platform: Sustained Success Through Continuous Evaluation, Adaptation, And Engagement:**

An author's platform is pivotal to their success in the current digital landscape. It encompasses the author's online presence, social media networks, website, email list, and various promotional activities. However, building a successful author platform is not a one-time task; it requires continuous evaluation, adaptation to new technologies or trends, and long-term engagement with readers. This section aims to provide insights on how authors can nurture and evolve their platform to achieve sustained success.

**Evaluate Your Current Platform:**

Regularly assessing the effectiveness of your platform is vital. Consider these aspects:

**Website:** Is your website user-friendly, visually appealing, and optimized for mobile devices?

**Social Media:** Are your social media profiles consistent, regularly updated, and engaging for your target audience?

**Email List:** How active is your email list, and are you providing valuable content to your subscribers?

**Analytics:** Utilize various analytical tools to measure website traffic, engagement rates, and social media metrics to gain insights into your audience's preferences.

**Stay Aware of New Technologies and Trends:**

Innovation and technology are constantly evolving, and as an author, staying updated is crucial. Consider:

**Social Media Platforms:** Be aware of emerging social media platforms and understand which ones align with your target audience. Experiment with new platforms with potential to reach a wider audience.

**Automation Tools:** Explore automation tools like email marketing software, scheduling apps for social media posts, or chatbots to streamline your promotional efforts and enhance efficiency.

**Virtual Events:** Stay up to date with the latest trends in virtual events such as webinars, live Q&A sessions, or online book clubs. These events can help you connect directly with readers, show your knowledge, and grow your audience.

**Focus on Long-term Engagement:**

Building a strong connection with your readers is vital for sustained success. Consider these strategies:

**Content Strategy:** Continuously provide valuable and engaging content through blog posts, articles, videos, or podcasts related to your writing, genre, or author journey. Focus on creating a community of loyal readers who appreciate your work and interact with them through comments, discussions, or live sessions.

**Personalization:** Tailor your communication and engagement efforts to your readers' preferences. Address their feedback, respond to comments, participate in discussions, and involve them in your writing process by seeking input on cover designs or character names.

**Author-Reader Events:** Organize virtual or physical events such as book signings, live readings, or interactive workshops to connect directly with your readers. These events not only strengthen your relationship with fans but also create memorable experiences that lead to word-of-mouth recommendations.

Nurturing and evolving your author platform is an ongoing process that requires continuous evaluation, adaptation to new technologies or trends, and long-term engagement with readers. By regularly evaluating your platform, staying aware of emerging technologies, and focusing on reader engagement, you can achieve sustained success as an author. Remember, the key is to consistently provide value and foster connections with your audience, leading to an ever-growing and supportive community around your work.

**Nurturing Reader Relationships:**

The significance of reader engagement cannot be overstated. In the digital age, where countless books, blogs, and articles vie for attention, engaging with readers has become a crucial part of building a loyal and dedicated fan base. By creating a personal connection and making readers feel heard and valued, authors not only increase their readership but also form a community of devoted followers.

First, engaging with readers establishes a personal connection that transcends the mere transactional relationship between author and reader. Through comments sections on blogs or social media platforms, authors can respond to readers' thoughts and opinions, sparking meaningful conversations. This two-way interaction humanizes the author and lets readers feel a sense of connection and empathy toward them. By building this emotional bond, readers become invested in the author's work, eagerly awaiting new releases and supporting the author by sharing their work with friends and family.

Engaging with readers makes them feel heard and valued. When authors take the time to respond to comments, address concerns, or acknowledge positive feedback, it sends a powerful message that readers' opinions matter. By listening and engaging in dialogue, authors show their commitment to their audience's satisfaction, which fosters a sense of loyalty. Readers who feel valued are more likely to become loyal fans, promoting the author's work and forming a community around it.

Reader engagement also creates a space for fans to connect with one another. By encouraging discussion and dialogue among readers, authors help with the formation of a community that shares common interests and passions. This community becomes a platform for readers to support and uplift one another, further cementing their allegiance to the author. In this community, readers not only celebrate the author's work but also engage in conversations about related topics, creating a sense of belonging and fostering a deeper connection with the author and their body of work.

Through reader engagement, authors gain valuable insights into their audience's preferences, desires, and expectations. By listening to readers' feedback, authors can fine-tune their writing, making sure it resonates with their fan base. This feedback loop is invaluable for authors seeking to grow and improve their craft. Additionally, by incorporating reader suggestions and involving them in the creative process, authors make their fans feel like valued collaborators, further strengthening their loyalty and dedication.

Reader engagement holds immense significance for authors in building a loyal and dedicated fan base. By engaging with readers, authors create a personal connection that goes beyond the transactional relationship. Making readers feel heard and valued fosters loyalty, promotes positive word-of-mouth recommendations, and creates a community of devoted followers. Reader engagement provides authors with crucial insights and feedback, enabling them to refine their writing and build stronger connections with their audience. So, authors should focus on reader engagement as a vital part of their work to develop a passionate and dedicated fan base.

### Building Relationships Through Communication:

In the digital age, communication has become easier and more accessible than ever before. This has opened countless opportunities for authors to connect with their readers in meaningful ways. Building relationships through effective communication is an essential part of developing a loyal and dedicated fan base.

One method of communication that has become increasingly popular among authors is the use of social media platforms. With billions of active users worldwide, platforms such as Facebook, Twitter, and Instagram offer a direct line of communication between authors and their readers. By engaging in conversations, sharing updates, and responding to comments, authors can foster a sense of community and make their readers feel valued and heard.

Author websites also play a crucial role in building relationships with readers. A well-designed and user-friendly website can serve as a hub where readers can find information about the author, their books, and upcoming events. Interactive features, such as discussion forums or Q&A sections, can encourage readers to actively engage with the author and each other. Many authors maintain a blog on their website, providing readers with valuable content and a platform for ongoing dialogue.

Newsletters are another effective tool for fostering reader engagement. By offering exclusive content, such as sneak peeks, behind-the-scenes insights, or bonus material, authors can provide added value to their readers. Sending regular newsletters not only keeps readers informed but also creates a sense of exclusivity, strengthening the bond between author and reader.

The significance of reader engagement cannot be overstated. By connecting with readers, authors can create a personal connection that goes beyond the pages of their books. Readers often appreciate the opportunity to interact with their favorite authors, ask questions, and share their thoughts on the work. By responding to comments, participating in discussions, or attending book clubs, authors can make readers feel like an integral part of their literary journey.

Engaging with readers also directly affects building a loyal and dedicated fan base. When readers feel valued and heard, they are more likely to become repeat customers, eagerly expecting each new release. They are more likely to recommend the author's work to others, increasing the author's reach and potential audience.

Effective communication tools such as social media, author websites, and newsletters provide authors with powerful means to connect with readers and foster a sense of community. By engaging with readers, authors can build personal connections, make readers feel valued, and ultimately create a loyal and dedicated fan base.

**Creating A Sense of Community:**

Creating a sense of community around a book or author can have many benefits for both the readers and the author. By offering exclusive content, organizing virtual events, and helping with reader discussions, a community can be fostered, letting readers feel a sense of belonging and encouraging interaction with the author and other like-minded readers. This can lead to increased engagement, a more dedicated fanbase, and ultimately, a stronger bond between the author and their readers.

One way to create a sense of community is by offering exclusive content. This can be as bonus chapters, character profiles, or behind-the-scenes insights into the writing process. By providing access to this exclusive content, readers feel valued and gain a deeper understanding of the book and its author. This fosters a sense of belonging within the community, as they share a unique connection through this additional material.

Organizing virtual events is another effective way to create a community. This can include author Q&A sessions, virtual book launches, or live readings. Virtual events let readers interact with the author directly, ask questions, and gain insights into the inspirations behind the book. These events bring readers together, letting them connect with one another and establish a sense of community.

Helping with reader discussions is a crucial part of building a sense of community. This can be achieved through online book clubs or forums where readers can share their thoughts, interpretations, and favorite moments from the book. By creating a platform for readers to engage in meaningful conversations, a shared experience is created, further reinforcing their sense of belonging within the community.

The benefits of creating a sense of community around a book or author are numerous. First, it encourages reader interaction and engagement, leading to a more active and dedicated fan base. Readers who feel connected to a community are more likely to spread the word about the book and engage in word-of-mouth marketing.

Second, a sense of community fosters a deeper connection between the author and their readers. This connection has the potential to transform readers into loyal fans, eagerly expecting future works and supporting the author's career.

Last, by creating a community, readers can connect with like-minded individuals who share their passion for the author's work. This sense of belonging can be immensely rewarding, providing readers with a space to express their thoughts and feelings about the book, fostering relationships, and even leading to lasting friendships.

Creating a sense of community around a book or author offers many benefits for both readers and authors. By offering exclusive content, organizing virtual events, and helping with reader discussions, a community can be fostered, letting readers feel a sense of belonging and encouraging interaction. This engagement leads to increased loyalty, a stronger bond between author and readers, and an enriched reading experience for all involved.

## Understanding Reader Preferences:

Understanding reader preferences is crucial for authors looking to effectively engage and connect with their audience. In today's era of information overload, where countless books, articles, and blogs are readily available, it is essential to stand out and create content that resonates with readers. This is where listening to reader feedback and understanding their preferences becomes invaluable.

By seeking and listening to reader feedback, authors can gain insights into what works and what doesn't. Readers are the ultimate critics, and their opinions are a goldmine of information that can guide authors to tailor their content. Understanding reader preferences lets authors craft stories, articles, or blog posts more compelling and appealing to their target audience.

Tailoring content to match reader preferences creates a stronger bond between authors and their readers. When readers find content that aligns with their tastes and interests, they are more likely to become loyal fans. They feel understood and appreciated, which fosters a sense of connection and trust. This bond becomes the foundation for a long-lasting relationship, where readers eagerly anticipate new releases and eagerly recommend the author's work to others.

Listening to reader feedback and understanding their preferences also enables authors to evolve and grow as writers. Constructive criticism lets authors improve their storytelling, writing style, and even their genre focus. It pushes authors out of their comfort zones and encourages them to experiment with new ideas or genres while still catering to the desires of their readers.

However, it is important for authors to balance acknowledging reader preferences and maintaining their own voice and vision. As much as it is critical to meet reader expectations, authors should not solely rely on them. They should also trust their instincts and stay true to their creative vision. A healthy blend of audience insights and personal expression ultimately leads to creating authentic and engaging content.

Understanding reader preferences is vital for authors aiming to establish a strong connection with their audience. By listening to reader feedback and adapting their content authors can craft stories that resonate with their readers on a deeper level. This understanding not only strengthens the bond between authors and readers but also lets authors grow and evolve as writers. So, embrace reader preferences, and let them guide you toward becoming a writer who captivates and inspires their audience.

### Providing A Personalized Reading Experience: Making Readers Feel Special

In today's digital age, where readers are spoiled for choice with an overwhelming number of books, it has become essential for authors to engage their audience on a personal level. By providing a personalized reading experience, authors can not only make readers feel special but also encourage their continued support. This section explores various ways authors can do this, including bonus content, special acknowledgments, and personalized messages.

### Bonus Content:

Including bonus content alongside the main narrative is an excellent way to enhance the reading experience and make readers feel valued. Authors can include more chapters, epilogues, or alternative endings exclusively for readers who buy the book or support the author on specific platforms. This special content rewards readers for their loyalty and fosters a deeper connection with the author's work.

### Special Acknowledgments:

Authors can acknowledge their readers in a unique and heartfelt manner. Including a special acknowledgments section at the end of a book lets authors express their gratitude directly, mentioning readers who have provided support and feedback. This personal touch not only makes the individuals mentioned feel appreciated but also encourages others to strive for recognition, further supporting the author's work.

## Personalized Messages:

Another way authors can personalize the reading experience is by incorporating personalized messages. This can involve a handwritten note in the book, digital messages tailored to each reader, or even direct communication through social media platforms or email newsletters. By contacting readers individually, authors show a genuine connection and foster a sense of exclusivity, further engaging readers and encouraging their ongoing support.

## Reader Feedback:

Authors can actively seek feedback from their readers, showing their opinions are valuable. This can be done through surveys, Q&A sessions, or author-led book club discussions. Using reader feedback, authors can provide a more tailored reading experience, addressing specific interests and concerns of their audience. Additionally, acknowledging and starting suggestions from readers further reinforces their importance and strengthens the author-reader relationship.

## Interactive Platforms:

Authors can leverage interactive platforms to enhance the reading experience. Creating exclusive online communities or forums enables readers to connect with one another and the author, fostering a sense of belonging and camaraderie. By participating in these communities, authors can provide a more personal reading experience and build a loyal reader base that actively supports their work.

Providing a personalized reading experience is a powerful way for authors to make readers feel special and encourage their continued support. By offering bonus content, special acknowledgments, personalized messages, seeking reader feedback, and using interactive platforms, authors can establish a strong connection with their audience. This personal touch not only lets authors express gratitude but also creates a loyal and engaged reader base that eagerly expects and supports their future endeavors.

. . .

## The Power of Positive Word-Of-Mouth: Boosting an Author's Success:

In today's competitive publishing landscape, authors are constantly seeking effective ways to promote their work and build a loyal readership. Amidst the noise of online marketing and paid advertisements, one avenue stands out for its authenticity and potential impact: positive word-of-mouth. When satisfied readers recommend an author's work to others, it can significantly contribute to their success. In this section, we will explore the power of positive word-of-mouth and provide strategies for authors to encourage readers to share their enthusiasm and recommendations with others.

### Deliver a Stellar Reading Experience:

The foundation of positive word-of-mouth lies in the quality of the written work itself. Authors must strive to create an exceptional reading experience that captivates and resonates with their audience. By crafting well-developed characters, compelling storylines, and immersive settings, authors can leave a lasting impression on readers and inspire them to share their enjoyment with friends, family, and online communities.

### Engage with Readers:

Building a meaningful relationship with readers is crucial for fostering positive word-of-mouth. Authors can achieve this by engaging with their audience through various channels. Participating in book clubs, literary events, and social media platforms lets authors establish a personal connection, listen to feedback, and reciprocate readers' enthusiasm. Engaging with readers not only increases the likelihood of positive word-of-mouth but also cultivates a loyal fanbase.

### Leverage Book Reviews:

Book reviews play a pivotal role in influencing readers' purchasing decisions. Encouraging satisfied readers to leave reviews on popular platforms like Goodreads, Amazon, or book blogs can significantly affect an author's success. Authors can tactfully remind readers to leave a review at the end of their book, through newsletters, or by using social media incentives, such as giveaways or exclusive content. Positive reviews act as powerful testimonials, attracting new readers and confirming the author's credibility.

**Harness the Power of Influencers:**

In a digital age driven by social media, influencers hold immense sway over consumer behavior. By partnering with influencers who align with their genre or target demographic, authors can tap into new audiences and enhance positive word-of-mouth. Providing influencers with advanced reader copies, hosting virtual author events, or collaborating on content creation can generate buzz and promote readership. Influencers' recommendations carry weight and can significantly affect an author's visibility and sales.

**Create Shareable Content:**

Authors can actively encourage readers to spread the word by creating shareable content. This could include quote graphics, book trailers, interactive quizzes, or behind-the-scenes glimpses into their writing process. By making these assets easily shareable on social media platforms, authors can leverage readers' enthusiasm and amplify positive word-of-mouth. Additionally, running contests or challenges where readers are encouraged to share their love for the author's work with their own networks can exponentially increase reach and engagement.

Positive word-of-mouth remains a potent force in the success of an author. By focusing on the delivery of a stellar reading experience, engaging with readers, leveraging book reviews, harnessing the power of influencers, and creating shareable content, authors can encourage and amplify positive recommendations from satisfied readers. The power of word-of-mouth lies not only in its potential to attract new readers but also in fostering a strong connection between an author and their audience, leading to long-term success and growth in their writing career.

**Chapter Summary:**

The chapter discusses the importance of building authenticity and trust with readers by sharing personal stories, being transparent, and creating relatability.

Engaging with readers on social media through live sessions, give-aways, responding to comments, and exclusive content is highlighted.

Email marketing enables direct communication, exclusive content, updates, and personalization. In-person events and book signings let authors connect directly with readers.

Leveraging reader feedback and reviews helps improve future works and shows appreciation. Collaborating with influencers and fellow authors expands reach and taps into existing audiences.

Creating a sense of community encourages engagement and advocacy. Understanding reader preferences through feedback provides insights to resonate with the audience.

Personalized experiences like bonus content and acknowledgments make readers feel valued. Positive word-of-mouth through stellar books, engagement, reviews, influencers, and shareable content can significantly boost an author's success.

Overall, the chapter outlines strategies for building connections with readers, helping with interactions, expressing gratitude, gaining insights into their preferences, and leveraging advocates to nurture relationships.

# CONCLUSION

**Realize Your Potential Through Self-Publishing:**

As we conclude this comprehensive guide, you now have the tools and knowledge to write, publish, and market your self-published book. By applying the techniques covered in this book, you can craft compelling stories, publish professionally, spread your message widely, and establish your authority.

**Let's Recap the Key Ideas:**

- Tap into your unique voice and perspective to write an authentic and resonant story. Structure your ideas logically and edit vigorously to create a high-quality manuscript.
- Design an appealing cover and interior, distribute through a variety of channels, and market effectively to connect with readers who will value your book.
- View your book not just as a standalone product but as a platform and springboard to grow your personal brand and strengthen your business or career.

- Build relationships with your readers, collaborate with others, and continuously nurture your author platform for long-term success.

While self-publishing presents immense opportunities, it also requires commitment and a strategic approach. By implementing the advice in this book, you can avoid common pitfalls and maximize your chances of succeeding and thriving as an author.

Believe in the significance of your ideas and the difference your book can make in the world. Commit to consistency and continuous learning on your self-publishing journey. The rewards of sharing your story far outweigh the effort required.

You now have everything you need to self-publish successfully. All that remains is acting. Have faith in your voice, craft your story carefully, and boldly put it out into the world. You have the potential to enlighten minds, inspire others, and leave a lasting legacy. Your story deserves to be heard.

It's time to realize your full potential through self-publishing. We wish you the best in your writing endeavors and look forward to seeing the impact your published book will make. Keep writing, dreaming, and changing lives.

# ABOUT THE AUTHOR

Rae A. Stonehouse is a Canadian born author & speaker.

His professional career as a Registered Nurse working predominantly in psychiatry/mental health, spanned four decades.

Rae has embraced the principal of CANI (Constant and Never-ending Improvement) as promoted by thought leaders such as Tony Robbins and brings that philosophy to each of his publications and presentations.

He has dedicated the latter segment of his journey through life to overcoming his personal inhibitions. As a 25+ year member of Toastmasters International he has systematically built his self-confidence and communicating ability. He is passionate about sharing his lessons with his readers and listeners.

His publications thus far are of the personal & professional development, self-help, self-improvement genre and systematically offer valuable sage advice on a specific topic. His writing style can be described as being conversational.

As an author Rae strives to have a one-to-one conversation with each of his readers, very much like having your own personal self-development coach.

Rae is known for having a wry sense of humor that features in his publications. To learn more about Rae A. Stonehouse, visit the Wonderful World of Rae Stonehouse at https://raestonehouse.com.

## CHAPTER SIXTEEN

# ALSO, BY RAE A. STONEHOUSE

V<small>ISIT</small>   <small>HTTPS://LIVEFOREXCELLENCE.STORE/</small>   for   a   selection   of personal/professional self-development books by Rae A. Stonehouse.

If you have found this book to be helpful, please leave us a warm review wherever you purchased it.

You may be interested in *The Successful Self-Publisher Series:*

**Book One: Writing & Publishing as a Business**

Self-publishing can be frustrating to learn, but author Rae A. Stonehouse's *Successful Self-Publisher Series* offers advice on writing, publishing, and marketing your own book. The series covers topics such as organizing your content, formatting your manuscript, and creating book titles that sell.

**Book Two: Self-Publishing for Fun and Profit**

The Successful Self Publisher Series, Book Two: Self-Publishing for Fun and Profit, by author Rae A. Stonehouse, offers advice on self-publishing, covering topics such as proofreading, pricing, royalties, and digital rights management. The book is part of a series that also includes a guide on writing and publishing as a business and one on content marketing strategies.

### Book Three Content Marketing Strategies That Work

Writing a book can take up to 30% of your time, while marketing can take up to 130%. However, marketing your content is achievable with basic and advanced strategies, as highlighted in the book "Content Marketing Strategies That Work" by author Rae A. Stonehouse.

All three books are available in e-book, paperback and audio versions. Visit our Live For Excellence online store at https://liveforexcellence.store/product-category/self-publishing/ for more details.

~

www.ingramcontent.com/pod-product-compliance
Lightning Source LLC
Chambersburg PA
CBHW061143120626
46546CB00005B/1911